1978

PERGAMON INTERNATIONAL LIBRARY
of Science, Technology, Engineering and Social Studies
The 1000-volume original paperback library in aid of education,
industrial training and the enjoyment of leisure
Publisher: Robert Maxwell, M.C.

ACTION WITH THE ELDERLY

THE PERGAMON TEXTBOOK
INSPECTION COPY SERVICE

An inspection copy of any book published in the Pergamon International Library will
gladly be sent to academic staff without obligation for their consideration for course
adoption or recommendation. Copies may be retained for a period of 60 days from
receipt and returned if not suitable. When a particular title is adopted or recommended
for adoption for class use and the recommendation results in a sale of 12 or more copies,
the inspection copy may be retained with our compliments. The Publishers will be
pleased to receive suggestions for revised editions and new titles to be published in this
important International Library.

PROBLEMS AND PROGRESS IN DEVELOPMENT

Editor: Jack Kahn

INTERNATIONAL JOURNAL OF NURSING STUDIES

An international journal concerned with the publication of papers on all aspects of nursing and allied professions throughout the world. The emphasis is on meeting the community's needs for all types of nursing care, on preparing young people for assuming nursing duties and responsibilities and on encouraging all aspects of nursing research.

ACTION
WITH THE ELDERLY

A Handbook for Relatives and Friends

KENNETH M. G. KEDDIE,

M.B., Ch.B., D.P.M., M.R.C.Psych.

Consultant Psychiatrist
Montrose, Tayside Health Board

Foreword by

Ivor R. C. Batchelor

C.B.E., F.R.S.E., M.B., Ch.B., F.R.C.P.E., F.R.C.Psych, D.P.M.

Professor of Psychiatry, University of Dundee

PERGAMON PRESS

OXFORD · NEW YORK · TORONTO · SYDNEY · PARIS · FRANKFURT

U.K.	Pergamon Press Ltd., Headington Hill Hall, Oxford OX3 0BW, England
U.S.A.	Pergamon Press Inc., Maxwell House, Fairview Park, Elmsford, New York 10523, U.S.A.
CANADA	Pergamon of Canada Ltd., 75 The East Mall, Toronto, Ontario, Canada
AUSTRALIA	Pergamon Press (Aust.) Pty. Ltd., 19a Boundary Street, Rushcutters Bay, N.S.W. 2011, Australia
FRANCE	Pergamon Press SARL, 24 rue des Ecoles, 75240 Paris, Cedex 05, France
FEDERAL REPUBLIC OF GERMANY	Pergamon Press GmbH, 6242 Kronberg/Taunus, Pferdstrasse 1, Federal Republic of Germany

First edition 1978

British Library Cataloguing in Publication Data

Keddie, Kenneth M G
Action with the elderly.—(Problems and progress in development).—(Pergamon international library).
1. Aged—Great Britain—Care and hygiene
I. Title II. Series
649.8   HV1481.G52   77-30667

ISBN 0-08-021442-8 Hard cover
ISBN 0-08-021441-X Flexicover

Printed Offset Litho in Great Britain by Cox & Wyman Ltd, Fakenham, Norfolk

Dedicated to E.A.K

Contents

List of Illustrations

Illustrated by Hilary Tottman (cartoons) and Tom King (photographs)

List of Photographs

Foreword

An increasing concern for the handicapped and the underprivileged which is being shown by the community is one of the most encouraging features of our troubled times. The difficulties of those growing old in a technological, mobile and rapidly changing society engage widespread sympathy, and much voluntary work is directed towards their alleviation. Relatives particularly want to know how best to assist the old person who needs help. There is much that is useful already in print, but it has been addressed to a variety of audiences and it is scattered. Here is a book of practical advice which is comprehensive, reliable, easy to read. It is intended primarily for relatives, friends and voluntary workers, but it could be read with profit also by many professional workers. Dr. Keddie's humane and sensible guide to preventing and coping with disability and to bringing effective help will, I am sure, be much appreciated and used.

Dundee, 1978   Ivor R. C. BATCHELOR

Editorial Introduction

The word "action" in the title of Dr. Keddie's book is a clear indication of his purpose. Intention to do good is valueless unless it is converted into practical procedures.

The topic is, nevertheless, a difficult one to present, because complex emotions underlie both the intentions and the procedures. Old people form an increasingly large proportion of the total population, and their care may appear to be an unwelcome burden on the active work force. At a personal level, there are those who carry resentment against family ties, through which the life of the young is limited by the claims of ever-present older members.

Insufficient emphasis is likely to be placed on the positive contribution that old people make to family life, and there is an unrealised capacity to do productive work within the community.

There is no lack of examples of old people who live independent lives, and who need no outside help beyond the unobtrusive courtesies that are still offered in our much maligned epoch. The large majority of old people live happily with their own families. They are a stabilising influence in the community, and they provide a link between the past, in which the present generation has its roots, and a future which is yet to be attained.

There are, however, large numbers of old people who are denied independence by bad social conditions, poverty, disabilities and ill-health. The number of those who need help exceeds the number of those who seek it. Independence of spirit may survive the actuality of diminishing resources.

Dr. Keddie writes comprehensively about the range of problems which are likely to occur.

The needs of old people are the same as those at any other age: medical treatment when ill; financial support when personal earnings and savings are insufficient; and improvement in housing accommodation and social conditions when they are unsatisfactory. Old people also need human contacts to replace the loss of family members and friends.

Every profession is called upon to supply some of those needs. The Health Service and Social Services Departments have been given (among their multitudinous tasks) specific responsibilities for the care of the old. The magic of the statutory instrument is not powerful enough to turn declared public policy into action for the benefit of the individuals who need help. The professional services have not been given either staff or resources to carry out these tasks. It will be necessary for goodwill to find expression through voluntary organisations and the individual concern of members of the public.

Professional and voluntary services are alike in the need of guidance at the point of contact with the recipient of help. Dr. Keddie's book is characterised throughout by its practicality: when to offer help, and when to stand by; how to find information that is not readily at hand; and how to get specialised services when they are needed.

The old person needs help that has the qualities of the good doctor, the good priest, the good neighbour and, even at advanced ages, there is a need for the qualities of the good parent. Dr. Keddie packs all these qualities into his volume, and he manages to convey (along with his common-sense practical messages) the personal respect which is the most essential ingredient of all.

It is a privilege to include the book in this series.

JACK KAHN

Publisher's Note

This is a book by a Scottish author based on his experiences in Scotland, but the subject it covers is relevant to the entire English-speaking world. No attempt has been made to distract the readers by adding local organisations and examples in parentheses or footnotes, but rather to encourage them to seek examples in their own locality. However, for the convenience of readers in the U.S.A. an appendix has been added giving the names and addresses of useful organisations.

The Author and the Publishers would like to record their thanks to all those who have helped in the compilation of this work. They would especially like to thank the photographic models, both human and animal!

CHAPTER 1

Independence in Old Age

Most retired people enjoy life to the full. Even more important, many elderly people continue for many long years to be active citizens in one way or another, demonstrating a high degree of responsibility and sense of duty towards other members of the community.

Old people treasure their independence. They guard it like a pot of gold. This is partly because in later years, our basic characteristics become more exaggerated. A person who has been sensitive all his life and fairly self-contained may wish to be left absolutely alone in old age. This is his privilege.

Let me put this another way. To want to be by oneself, when old, may be no more than evidence of personal idiosyncrasy.

Those wishing to help elderly people should, therefore, be aware that any old person living a rather isolated life is not necessarily ill or sick in the mind.

The best advice I can give you, when in doubt whether or not to offer assistance to any elderly man or woman, is to ask an expert: the family doctor, the health visitor, the social worker. When, however, an elderly person is ill or disturbed in any way, we are then dealing with a quite different problem. Disability, whatever else it does, restricts independence.

What to my mind is so heartening, in today's world, is the large number of remedies available to us to help old people cope with disability. Let me give some examples of this.

THE BLIND PERSON

This story concerns an eighty year old woman, living alone and trying to adapt to blindness of recent origin.

This old lady had become completely blind, six months previously, having had failing vision for the previous year or so. The neighbours were attentive and very kind. They did feel, however, that she was becoming rather senile and might require more care than they could give. The reason they gave was that the old women was very liable to start vacuum-cleaning her house at any hour of the night.

Following complaints from the neighbours, a social worker called. He considered that the old woman was quite clear in her mind. It was equally apparent that she had no ready means of knowing whether it was morning, afternoon, evening or night.

The social worker recommended that a telephone be installed in the house. This was done and as a result the old woman was able to dial for "time" whenever she wished. The episodes of disturbed behaviour became negligible after this.

AFTER HOSPITAL

An elderly man of seventy returned home after having a successful operation for a broken leg following a fall. From the medical point of view the old man was progressing very well. Unfortunately he had to cope not only with his own difficulties but that of his invalid wife. The couple lived in a two-storey house with sleeping and toilet accommodation upstairs and cooking facilities downstairs. For the preparation of a hot drink, the gas stove in the kitchen was used. This therefore meant that the old man, on coming home from hospital, had to make an undue number of trips upstairs and downstairs.

The family doctor called and noted the old man's feelings of agitation and general loss of confidence. The doctor suggested that the couple purchase an electric kettle, which the old man was able to use upstairs. In this way he prepared hot drinks, as well as soup with instant prepara-tions, without having to journey downstairs. This helped to improve the general situation.

FEAR OF ATTACK

Many old people are naturally apprehensive about going for walks or shopping in the late afternoon or early evening.

They have read of people being mugged and are afraid that next time they themselves may be the victim. To help overcome these anxieties, it may be a good idea to provide the old person with a portable alarm. Many of these are light and easy to operate. One type of alarm, mentioned on page 88, gives a loud buzz when a pin, attached to a long piece of thread, is removed. Such devices help to give old people a much needed sense of confidence.

These cases illustrate the practical approach that can be employed to ease an old person's burden and so make life not only tolerable, but also enjoyable again.

Optimism must be the watchword when dealing with any frail old person. Naturally this has to be tempered with down-to-earth reality, when the disability is serious and irreversible. To have suffered a major stroke, to be unable to control the bladder or to have severe arthritis is to be handicapped to a serious degree.

Subsequent chapters describe the various types of assistance available within the community for dealing with disability in old age.

Success in this sphere is, of course, entirely dependent on the willingness of people, like yourself, to get involved and to give a little of that most precious commodity—time.

CHAPTER 2

Helping in a Personal Way

SYMPATHY AND UNDERSTANDING

It is vitally important to be concerned for the welfare of the elderly frail. This means that you have to be interested in the elderly person in question and to be tolerant of any eccentric behaviour. Also, you must not be on the look-out for the usual rewards—the word of thanks, the cup of tea. It must be enough to know that you are trying to help.

THE FIRST MEETING

Some people are a little apprehensive when making that first contact with an elderly person. After all, it normally takes both time and a bit of effort to get on well with people, especially those we have not met before.

When people do meet for the first time they anticipate that there will be some initial awkwardness and embarrassment. By convention we use some socially acceptable ploy to break the ice. Most people rely on the weather. Others—more daring—talk about politics or sport. Likewise when you visit an old person for the first time, you could perhaps make conversation easy from the start by offering the old person something to read.

This could be a brochure or a magazine or even a book that has some relevance. In the case of a voluntary visitor from an official organisation a pamphlet illustrating the services provided might be appropriate. The first meeting, and this applies to any type of human relationship, is always a critical one. Bluntness, inquisitiveness and an excess of enthusiasm are inappropriate. None of these is right for starting something that can, and should, have much to offer both sides. Care, sensitivity and awareness are the key notes.

GETTING ON TOGETHER

Establishing a "good relationship" with a person is not therefore something that occurs automatically. How well people get on will depend on various factors, such as respective ages, shared ideas and identity of outlook on life. In older people there can be other barriers to successful communication. I refer to dullness of hearing, poor eyesight and even a mild degree of mental impairment. Any of these can prevent, at least in the initial stages, meaningful contact being established between an old person and a visitor.

VISITING

Your own attitude to the question of visiting is critical. This is the acid test of the whole business. How often you in fact visit any particular elderly person will depend on the circumstances, e.g., whether the person lives alone, whether there are interested relatives nearby and whether the district nurse is involved.

Visitors of whatever nature, whether friends, relatives or volunteers, help to reduce an old person's sense of isolation. An old person living alone will set great store by these visits. They are often key events in such a person's life. Family physicians have always been aware of the value of keeping in touch regularly with their house-bound patients. The G.P. may drop in once a month or more often, but the routine is from the patient's point of view regular and predictable. Such knowledge by itself provides a sense of relief and comfort.

Old people are in a vulnerable position. They do not understand when a visitor's routine goes from a very generous three times a week visit to a leisurely call once every three months. In such circumstances the visits should not have started at all. The old person gets hurt and experiences a feeling of abandonment.

In essence then, one of the visitor's principal aims is to be continually interested in, and concerned for, each of the old people being visited.

Can visits ever harm an old person? The answer is simply, "Yes, at times". This would happen where permission for visiting had not been granted by the old person concerned or where the visitor and the old person were "ill-matched" because of a clash of personalities.

VOLUNTARY ORGANISATIONS

In organisations, such as the Red Cross,[1]* the Women's Royal Voluntary Service (W.R.V.S.),[2] and Old People's Welfare Committees there exists a convener responsible for any visiting scheme. The matching process is her responsibility and a very important one. The convener would also be available for general guidance, e.g. on advising about the optimum frequency of visits in any particular case.

The convener has to see that the voluntary visiting is done efficiently and is well co-ordinated. To ensure this, it is necessary to keep good records. Periodic assessment visits, of a tactful and informal nature, have to be made by the convener to get first-hand impressions from the old people of the service being provided. This information and the reports from the visitors themselves enable the convener to tell (a) which categories of old people should be visited and (b) what should be the nature of the visit in each type of case.

Recently the W.R.V.S.[2] started a most worthy Good Companions Scheme in several parts of the country. Here, help of a practical nature is given on a regular basis to handicapped and aged people who are finding it increasingly difficult to cope on their own. The Good Companion may clean windows, go shopping or even escort the old person to hospital for an outpatient appointment.

Assistance may not necessarily be given on a long term basis. The Good Companionship Scheme provided for say six weeks can often enable a person to leave hospital earlier than would otherwise be possible.

---

* Superscript numbers indicate that additional information can be found in the Chapter Notes at the end of the book.

REACTIONS FROM THE ELDERLY

The success or failure of any visiting scheme is determined in large measure by the attitudes of both the old people and the visitors.

Let us look at some of the reactions an old person may have when asked whether he would like to be visited regularly. In most cases the old person is very welcoming. Indeed, he is usually relieved that there is somebody who is understanding and to whom he can turn for companionship and also for competent guidance. Some other people—and this usually represents only a minority of cases—are quite emphatic that they wish to be left alone. The visitor would then, of course, diplomatically withdraw from the scene, possibly saying, "Don't forget to contact us later on, if you wish". Lastly, there are quite a number of old people who are rather wavering. They realise that, because of frailty, they need help in one form or another. They will feel equally strongly that they wish to retain their independence and this feeling results in a half-hearted rejecting attitude.

Which particular old people are most likely to appreciate and benefit from visits? Probably at the top of any list would be those who have been recently bereaved. Also important are those people living alone, who are unable to get out much. We should make a particular effort with old people who have been re-housed or who have recently returned home after a stay in hospital.

REACTIONS FROM VISITORS

Many voluntary visitors experience difficulty, at least in the initial stages, in getting on with elderly people. This is because of the prejudices that all of us have about the old and the frail. To be more specific, each of us has an instinctive fear of experiencing, both in ourselves and in others, physical and mental decline. In addition, frailty in others reminds us of our own vulnerability—of the inevitability of our own ageing. Quite often too, visitors feel overwhelmed when faced with an old person with problems that are complex and seemingly intractable.

GIVING PRESENTS

Is it good policy when visiting an old person to take something along? There is no doubt that it helps to cement a relationship if, on the first visit, something tangible (like a pot of jam or flowers) is handed over. This should not, however, become a regular feature of visiting, as it is liable to make the old person feel beholden to the visitor. It may be rather financially embarrassing as well. For some old people it is quite a good idea to take along a copy of the local newspaper. In many cases one can

A newspaper is always welcome

provide a considerable amount of enjoyment by reading out items of local gossip to the old person.

In order to express their appreciation to a visitor, an old person will often want to be hospitable by offering a cup of tea. Good manners, as well as common sense, dictates that you accept such an offer even if you have misgivings about a lack of hygiene in the kitchen.

THE AIMS OF VISITING

Let us now consider the various ways in which an elderly person can benefit from your visits:

(a) Obviously the visitor attempts to provide the old person with companionship. Often this is all that is necessary.

(b) Practical help in one form or another can be given. The various things that can be done are mentioned in other parts of this book.

(c) As a visitor, one is in a good position to help to keep the old person up to date with helpful information. You may well be able to give news of the opening of a luncheon club, new pension rates and concessionary fares on public transport.

(d) Particularly in old people who live alone, visits can add an extra dimension. They give the old person something nice to think about. A life, that might otherwise be rather dull, takes on a different complexion.

(e) The fact that somebody is visiting an old person means plainly that that person has at least one human being who is interested in him. This helps to maintain the old person's self-respect.

(f) Where an old person has worries of one sort or another the opportunity to ventilate feelings to an outsider is often appreciated. As we all know, a problem that is shared is easier to bear. If the visitor is a good listener, the old person is more likely to arrive at practical solutions to his problems.

(g) In some cases, particularly with old people who are ill, the visitor provides a sense of reassurance by just being there. Often it is sufficient to sit silently, saying little.

POINTS TO BEAR IN MIND

If at all possible keep the visiting on a regular basis. It helps the old person if he knows when the next visit is due. If the visitor is unable to visit at the time arranged because of illness or a holiday, this information should be conveyed as soon as possible, e.g. by a postcard.

Don't assume, as many people do, that the wealthy people in the community who live in "splendid isolation" would not appreciate visits. Many old people who chance to be rich are also very lonely.

Many young mothers undertake visiting. It should be remembered that there are some old people who find toddlers and infants rather irritating. They are not so upset usually by the pram stage.

Small children may not always be welcome

The ability to visit an old person with a view to providing support is not the prerogative of one sex or of any particular age group. What is so exciting and challenging is that men, women, school children, students, the middle-aged and the recently retired all have a part to play.

THAT PERSONAL TOUCH

You should always be careful to respect the personalities of the people you visit. The elderly are individuals like everyone else. Their birthdays and other special days should be remembered. So do try and make the effort to send birthday cards and Christmas cards.

Women appreciate having a hair-do whatever their age. It is a great morale booster. Perhaps you can arrange for transport to take those you visit to the local hairdresser.

CONVERSATION

We all like to fill our time with interesting, worthwhile matters. It is no different for the elderly. The prime need in this regard is for conversation. We must allow our elderly folk to reminisce. Sometimes, of course, the elderly person will become a little repetitive and then that is the cue for the listener to change the topic.

HUMOUR

The visitor must always be prepared to introduce an element of humour into any conversation. There is always some item of local gossip that is good for a laugh! Sometimes the national news can be a bit gloomy and to offset this the telling of a suitable funny story could be good medicine.

SUSPICION

Interspersed with normal conversation there may be the occasional remark denoting suspicion. Where hearing or sight is a little faulty, it is natural for misunderstandings to arise at times. Conversations may be imperfectly understood and the entirely wrong meaning put on something.

BIZARRE IDEAS

Having said this, some old people do get bizarre ideas. These are delusions and are, by definition, false ideas that the person clings to with great tenacity. They may imagine, for example, that they are being persecuted by neighbours.

The ideas may be even stranger and involve, for example, Russian spies or radar traps set up by the police. Less commonly these funny ideas involve ideas of grandeur—the person thinks he or she has an exalted status. They start making pronouncements about being of royal blood. Conversely, well-to-do people may suddenly get the idea that they are impoverished.

The visitor should be tactful in handling such situations. Do not attempt to argue with an old person about these odd ideas. Try rather to put the idea into the background by conversation of a general nature.

At times the ideas become very odd and very persistent. The old person concerned may then start to bother the police or consult a solicitor. That is the time for the family doctor's advice to be sought.

Perhaps the family doctor, too, is caught in the web of suspicion. The old person will instruct you, "On no account go near that man—he's wicked and is trying to cause my downfall". It is usually best in these circumstances to take a calculated risk of offending the old person and informing the G.P. of what is going on.

LEISURE

We now realise how important it is for retired people to use their leisure time in a constructive manner. There should be continual efforts to widen horizons and to refresh impressions. Dr. Irene Gore feels that this is a very crucial theme. She elaborates her ideas in an excellent book, *Age and Vitality—Commonsense Ways of Adding Life to Your Years*. Old people can preserve, and also extend, their mental vitality by keeping in touch with contemporary trends and events.[3]

OUT AND ABOUT

Walks should be encouraged. They are a most relaxing pastime and beneficial to the health. Also, apart from the need to replace shoe leather, a walk costs nothing. When out for a walk old people are helping themselves in another less obvious way. Exposure to the sun encourages the skin to manufacture vitamin D for our needs. A good supply of this vitamin ensures that our bones remain healthy and strong.

Old people should never be reluctant to use a walking stick when out walking. It is often wise for a walking stick to have a rubber tip. This helps to prevent slips on wet pavements.

There is available a rather ingenious "Gadabout Chair". This is a durable Nylon seat on an aluminium tubular frame and only weighs $3\frac{1}{2}$ lb. It folds quickly and easily into a walking stick. The "Gadabout Chair" is a very handy aid for elderly people who wish to continue the more adventurous type of exercises, such as beach picnics with grandchildren.[4]

When out walking elderly people should make sure that they take care when crossing roads. They should be reminded to cross at a place where they can see and be seen. At night, something white should be worn. Alternately, armbands that are fluorescent and reflective could be worn. These can be obtained from The Royal Society for the Prevention of Accidents.[5] Another solution available to elderly people apprehensive about crossing roads in the dark is the Emer Flash. This is a rod a foot long and one inch in diameter. When it is switched on a series of brilliant amber flashes is produced at a rate of three a second.[6]

CLUBS

Helping old people to exercise their minds enables them to retain a youthful outlook on life. Where possible old people should be encouraged to leave their home to attend pensioners' clubs, Women's Guild meetings and the like. Arranging for a car to collect an old person to attend such meetings may form a most important part of a visitor's work. Such is the nature of community life today that transport, in one form or another, represents a lifeline to the elderly.

Occasionally you might want to organise a tea party, either at your home or elsewhere, for a small number of old people. They would be sure to have lots to talk about! There exists a national voluntary organisation, Contact, that has undertaken such work for the past ten years. The same group of old people, up to twelve in number, meets once a month for afternoon tea. Several volunteers are available to act as hostesses, so a succession of different houses are visited throughout the year.[7]

HOBBIES AND GAMES

Whether or not the old person is confined to his home, efforts should be made to encourage an interest in pursuits such as knitting or craft work. Many people regrettably do not discover their creative talents until they retire. Then—alas, only then—do they experience the joy of knitting

Don't forget the creative talents

a scarf for a football fan, making a pair of cleverly carved book ends or composing a simple poem, and this certainly combats the feeling of "being useless" of which so many old people complain.

Remember that, to a greater or less degree, there exists in every elderly person hidden talents. Grandma Moses was an old lady when she learned to paint and look what she achieved. "Art"—which no longer means work done solely with oil paint or water colours—can be a most satisfying pursuit for people of all ages.

Games, such as dominoes, cards, draughts, ludo or even scrabble, can provide many hours of stimulating diversion for the elderly person. Young people wanting to help the elderly in the community can often be involved in activities such as these. A profitable and pleasant way of spending time with an older person is by introducing him to one or other of the several versions of the card game of Patience—also known as Solitaire.[8]

A recently published book, *Games you Make and Play*, gives details of popular board games and also those that are overdue for a revival.[9]

Simple measures can sometimes be adopted to enable an elderly frail person to continue enjoying a game of cards. A rubber band round a pencil gives a better grip for score keeping. Special card holders that holds a hand of cards upright on the table may be necessary—an upturned plastic scrubbing brush could be used for this purpose.

LETTER WRITING

Several organisations exist to alleviate the isolation of the elderly and also the relatives caring for them. One of these is Wider Horizons. The focal point of this association is the magazine, which is published six times a year and the articles for which are all written by members. Wider Horizons has a flourishing pen-friend scheme which has recently been extended to include the exchange of tapes.[10]

Friends by Post, likewise, exists to help old people maintain contact with the outside world.[11]

The British Correspondence Chess Association is for those who are housebound but wish to pursue an interest in chess.[12]

TELEVISION AND RADIO

Most people today, young and old, enjoy watching television and also listening to the radio. On your visits you should make sure that your friend's television or radio is in fact working. It is usually a very simple and inexpensive matter to get a repair done. Enormous pleasure will result once the job is done. The local radio stations operating in some areas are particularly appreciated.

The Wireless for the Bedridden Society will, in appropriate cases of need, provide television sets and transistor radios. Those who are eligible for the scheme do not have to be either housebound or bedridden.[13] Often a local charity, e.g. the Old People's Welfare Committee, provides television sets for elderly people. Where there is financial hardship, the Society would be prepared to meet the cost of rental, maintenance and even the T.V. Licence.

Where noise from a radio might annoy other people in the house, an old person could use a set with an ear-piece.

Music lovers can also obtain endless hours of pleasure from a record player. Many of these are moderately cheap.

HOLIDAYS

Many hotels offer off-season holidays at reduced cost. Social services departments (social work departments in Scotland) and often local voluntary bodies—the Round Table, the Rotary, the Old People's Welfare Committee and the Red Cross—can organise these, either for individuals or groups. Even people requiring nursing care can be offered a break away from home in certain circumstances.

Suddenly the travel firms have realised that ten million retired people in Britain constitute an important market. This explains the special offers for the over-sixties in the field of inclusive holidays. Remarkably cheap deals are available for pensioners interested in either coach tours abroad or a holiday at a British resort.

Elderly people suffering from chest, heart or stroke illness, often benefit from a pleasant, restful holiday in a hotel or guest house which

Make sure the T.V. is working

provides the little extra care and the special facilities that are needed. To help with the planning of such a holiday The Chest and Heart Association has drawn up a booklet *Holiday addresses in Britain 1975*.[14]

Several other guides have been published giving information on holiday facilities for the disabled elderly.[15]

WORK AFTER RETIREMENT

Most people these days retire at a time when they are still enjoying comparatively good health. This means that many men and women, after leaving their employment on reaching retirement age, can undertake some alternative type of work. This helps to provide a continuing sense of purpose in the life of an old person.

Some retired people devote themselves to voluntary work, e.g. by helping in clubs and hospitals, visiting the handicapped and even taking a share of the inevitable committee work. There are several helpful books available for the would be volunteer.[16]

Others seek paid work, either through the advertising columns of newspapers or by applying at the local employment office. Usually, so far as retired men are concerned, there is a constant demand for gardeners, petrol-pump and car-park attendants and storemen.

Employment bureaux, run by commercial enterprises as well as voluntary organisations, have been set up in various parts of the United Kingdom to assist retired people in their quest for the right job. The Citizen's Advice Bureau will know if such an agency exists where you live.

There are Sheltered Work Centres available in some areas. These provide part-time light work for the elderly. If there is no Work Centre operating near you and you wish to enquire about the prospect of one being established, contact the Employment Fellowship.[17]

Keith Mossman has written a very stimulating book, *Looking Forward to Retirement*. This has an excellent chapter "Going back to Work", describing the range of work available to retired people. Mossman also has a section on hobbies. In this he gives a comprehensive list—from photography and painting to the collecting of pewter—of the many types of leisure tasks suitable for the elderly.[18]

A Guide to Activities for Older People by G. M. Gwyneth Wallis is another book on this theme. It aims to show what an immense variety of opportunities are open to people in their retirement.[19]

READING

For many people, the reading of a daily newspaper is an enjoyable and relaxing part of the day's routine. You should ensure that current newspapers and magazines are available. Don't forget, also, that many people appreciate being sent copies regularly of the particular local newspaper which serves the area in which they were brought up. Reading about familiar faces and places can be very stimulating for an old person.

LARGE-PRINT BOOKS

Remember that many libraries have specially made "large print" books that are useful for the old people with poor vision. Ulverscroft Large Print Books Ltd. will send direct to any member of the public any large print books that they produce. The firm will supply a current list of titles. *War and Peace* is now available in this form—in five volumes.[20]

In some areas the W.R.V.S. provide a "Books on Wheels" service for the elderly who are housebound. Normal and large print books are supplied.

Some public libraries are re-assessing the needs of older people, particularly those with failing eyesight. Many have installed records and cassettes that can be borrowed by ratepayers from all over the city. Books, plays, poetry and short stories are examples of spoken-word recordings that are available.

CASSETTES

Some people, because of illness, are unable to read or handle books in the ordinary way. They may join the National Listening Library, a charity that has built up a list of cassettes specially designed for a reproducer. This weighs 7 lb and is designed so that the majority of handicapped people can operate it without assistance. Headphones can be used in circumstances where the noise of the machine might upset or irritate other people. The cassettes range from the classics to all types of fiction and include archaeology, history and sport. The reading has been done by well-known actors and newscasters. Cassettes are sent in special containers which make posting easy.[21]

Blind people are not eligible for this. They have a comparable service provided by the Royal National Institute for the Blind.[22]

FAMILY

After a few visits to an old person's home you will be more aware of the family situation. The elderly person may often live with a relative— it could be husband or wife, brother, sister, son or daughter.

It is important to note which of the old person's family are a source of support to that person—whether or not they live in the same house. Many old people of course prefer to continue living alone, having their relatives at a reasonably close, but respectful distance.

PROBLEMS OF SHARING

Particular problems tend to arise where older people have to share a household with their children or grandchildren. There are three basic types of problems:

(a) Nursing

As a consequence of an old person's frailty, relatives may have to be on constant guard. They may have to prevent the old person falling, for example during a spell of restlessness at night. There may be other problems such as incontinence (lack of control of bladder or bowel). This type of burden is of course rendered much more bearable where there are regular visits from the district nurse or health visitors. At times the strain is sufficient to warrant the implementation of the hospital "six weeks in—six weeks out" scheme. This is where provision is made for an old person to have a spell in hospital, thereby giving the relatives time to recover. How to help an incontinent elderly relative is dealt with in more detail on page 82 and subsequent pages.

The Red Cross, in response to situations like this, have recently started short courses in "Nursing for the Family". Each course consists of four sessions on basic nursing skills. Members of the public can in this way learn how to make a person comfortable in bed, change a bottom sheet, lift a frail person in and out of a chair and such like.[23]

(b) Social

There are often financial difficulties. This is perhaps because a relative, usually a daughter, has to stay at home to look after an aged parent. Further problems arise because the relative concerned feels resentful both at the loss of freedom and the loss of income. There is an excellent organisation, the National Council for the Single Woman and her Dependants, which was founded to help single women who either have or have had responsibility for elderly or infirm relatives. The organisation basically provides a service of support and advice and has branches now in many parts of the United Kingdom—the addresses of these can be had from the Secretary.[24]

It is remarkable how often family problems occur simultaneously. An old woman's widowhood may coincide with her daughter's menopausal depression and also the grandchildren's exams, independence battles or broken love affairs. Such a situation is very explosive and needs sympathetic handling by those trying to help.

(c) *Psychological*

Difficulties of a psychological nature may easily arise where the person has a difficult personality. This can also occur where an insidious psychiatric disorder such as senility is developing. Elderly people usually resent the fact that, in their old age, they become increasingly dependent on their children. This naturally leads to frustration. A grandfather may then compensate for this feeling by upsetting household discipline. He could do this by taking the side of the grandchildren in any dispute. Alternatively he might act up in order to divert attention from the grandchildren.

RELATIVES HAVE PROBLEMS TOO

If you are visiting an old person who is being looked after by a relative, do not expect that particular relative to wait on you hand and foot. Your visit might well be the occasion for a relative to have a lie down or even do a little bit of shopping on her own.

Relationships within the older person's home, as within your own, are personal and private matters. Diplomacy and tact are often called for. An old person might invite an unsuspecting visitor to share hostile feelings about some family member. Be on your guard and always remain staunchly neutral in such circumstances.

HELP FROM NEIGHBOURS

The next door neighbour can be a key figure in the old person's life. Neighbours traditionally do not like to be seen interfering and therefore may appear to be rather shadowy figures. Most neighbours, however, are of a kindly disposition and would be prepared to provide help in a crisis. Where appropriate, therefore, it is often common sense to introduce oneself to such a neighbour. The visitor could leave an address or even a telephone number so that she could be contacted speedily.

CHAPTER 3

Helping in a Practical Way

GENERAL ASPECTS

You should try and check whether there are any little chores to be done. Quite often old people are reluctant to ask for help on the grounds that they do not want to be a bother to anyone.

Collecting a prescription, getting the weekly pension from the Post Office, taking the laundry to the launderette, changing a library book, cleaning the windows or even helping to write a letter are all examples of the practical help that can be given. Others are reading mail, setting the table, filling the coal bucket, chopping fire-wood and putting out the ashbin.

Talking of ashbins, some elderly people find them very difficult to move when full of refuse. The Director of Environmental Health, previously known as the Sanitary Inspector, will always be prepared to discuss any problems like this. The Director can be contacted at your District Council Offices or the town hall. A request for help would never be turned down. It could be arranged for the full ashbin to be uplifted from its usual place and then left empty at the kerbside.

One simple way of moving an ashbin a short distance unaided is by the use of a child's Baby Walker. These have four small wheels and an upright push-bar at one end. Provided the bin can be lifted on to the Baby Walker, it is then a matter of trundling the load to the collecting point.

COMPENSATING FOR MEMORY DIFFICULTIES

I have yet to meet the person with a perfect memory! Everyone has to rely to some extent on jotting things down. This habit of making shopping lists, writing down phone messages and noting down matters requiring early attention becomes increasingly important as we grow older. The visitor should therefore ensure that paper and pencil are in fact available for such a purpose.

PENSIONS ONLY
THIS WINDOW

Offer to collect a pension

Where the memory is faulty, a knowledge of the correct date can be impaired. Encouraging an old person to have a calendar can help with this problem. Scoring off the days regularly on the calendar can allow the old person to keep a check on time.

When an old person does suffer from memory trouble he is likely to find it difficult to cope with official forms. These can range from those claiming for extra pensions to those applying to get one's name on a housing list. In such instances the visitor should ensure that the old person understands the form and also fills it in correctly. In cases of doubt the visitors should always contact the social services department.

FOOD

Elderly people are often rather neglectful and slap dash about their diet. This may be in part because a person's appetite tends to diminish in later years. They may also do rather odd things such as catering for the family that has grown up and is living away from home. Some may, for the same reason, make pounds and pounds of jam that is never used. Again, too many loaves of bread may be bought and eventually the contents of the bread bin have to be fed to the birds.

We should try and ensure—in a tactful way—that an old person, particularly when living alone, has a reasonable amount of food in the house.

You must remember that some elderly people are not able to visit shops and some may not even be able to walk to the mobile vans.

Check there is plenty of food

AN ADEQUATE DIET

What constitutes an adequate diet for an old person? This of course will vary from person to person. Sufficient vitamins, proteins and calories generally must be taken to prevent faulty nutrition and hence bad health.

Ideally one should ensure that an old person each day gets:
    a reasonable helping of lean meat or fish
    a pint of milk
    a portion of cheese
    fresh or frozen green vegetables
    some fresh fruit
    some margarine.

When a person late in life is suddenly faced with the necessity of preparing food for himself, the resulting meals are liable to be monotonous and lack imagination. In circumstances such as this the purchase of *Easy Cooking for One or Two* by Louise Davies would be worthwhile.[1] Miss Davies is also responsible for producing a series of slide kits, including leaflets, to educate elderly people on nutrition. They may even be demonstrated in the home of a pensioner. Two of the topics are *An Emergency Food Store for the Elderly* and *Keeping Foods Fresh without a Refrigerator*. Miss Davies will send details on request.[2]

The W.R.V.S. has produced three enterprising and useful leaflets with recipes designed to provide much of the daily nutrition needed by the elderly. These leaflets are *Protein Providers*, *Sweet After-thoughts* and *Edible Extras*.[3]

It is also important to make sure that the old person can cope with the cooking facilities in his home. This is discussed in the section on "The Kitchen".

For many years now food manufacturers have produced convenience foods for babies and infants. Some of these firms are beginning to think at last of producing similar commodities for older people. This should certainly be a commercially viable enterprise.

Any elderly person, who is aware of an alteration in his weight, whether up or down, should be encouraged to report the matter to their family doctor.

PROVIDING FOR MEALS

Quite often an elderly person is fortunate enough to have some of his meals prepared for him and delivered at the door e.g. by that marvellous community service, Meals-on-Wheels. The old person may, for some reason, not take all the food provided. If this is a new development for the old person and if it persists, the matter should be reported to the local organiser of Meals-on-Wheels.

Some old people living alone arrange with neighbours in a similar position to take turns to prepare lunch for each other. This is a means of providing a little companionship at the same time.

In some areas there are luncheon clubs where the elderly person may eat a meal in convivial surroundings. Visits to these clubs should be encouraged. Information on the luncheon clubs in your area is available from the local branch of Age Concern, the Citizen's Advice Bureau or the Social Services departments. The Social Services departments will be listed in the telephone book under the name of the County or Metropolitan District Council.

COOKING BY GAS

Where a gas cooker is used, there should always be adequate ventilation. Leaking gas can constitute a serious hazard. A leak can arise from a fault in the cooker. This could be particularly dangerous to a person with an impaired sense of smell. Gas leaks carry a risk of explosion. Gas poisoning is an additional risk, where coal gas is used.

It is worth knowing that gas cookers fitted with safety devices can be bought or rented. The cost can be recovered from the social security department if the old person receives a supplementary pension. The department should be consulted before any purchase is made. A leaflet, *Gas Makes Living Easier*, has been produced by British Gas and describes the special fitments available for use with gas cookers. This leaflet, which is of relevance to both the elderly and the disabled, can be obtained from the Home Service Adviser for your local Gas Region.

Gas Boards in some areas offer regular free inspection of all gas appliances used by pensioners.

WARMTH

HOUSE INSULATION

Adequate heating is recognised to be a basic need in an old person's house. In addition, the cost of fuel has forced everyone to study the economics of house heating very closely. Several practical guides are available on this.[4] It can be a relatively easy matter to make a house better insulated—by the simple expedient of fitting inexpensive draught excluders at windows and doors. These can make an enormous difference.

Loft insulation can play a big part in preventing undue heat loss from a house. A quilt of insulating glass fibre or expanded polystyrene, two or three inches thick, in the roof space of a loft is a good investment. Another helpful tip—drawing thick curtains over a window at night can be as effective as double glazing as a method of conserving heat.

KEEPING WARM IN THE DAY

Old people tend to move around more slowly than those of younger age groups. They are therefore more liable to feel the cold. Some form of central heating is often ideal in such circumstances. In this way the dwelling is heated both safely and uniformly.

The type of clothes worn by an old person can determine whether or not they feel the cold. Clothing should be light, closely woven and not restricting.

Items like fur-lined slippers are of course expensive. Who knows, some kind fairy godmother might be around at the right moment to provide the cash!

Is there a sufficient supply of coal and logs available? If not—should more be ordered? The social security department may be able to help here, and in particular they will know if the old person is entitled to a special fuel allowance.[5] Payment schemes for old people for gas and electricity bills are available. Details of these may be obtained from local showrooms.

Age Concern produces a very informative leaflet *Warm up for Winter*.[6]

Keep warm in winter

FUEL COSTS

In cases of financial hardship a local authority may undertake, or assist with, heat insulation and improved heating of an old person's home.

Pensioners often have enormous financial difficulties as a result of high fuel costs.

To prevent accounts being built up it has been suggested that customers using electricity should be given the choice of alternative methods of payment. Pre-payment slot meters would be an ideal method for many old people. It therefore seems sad that several Electricity Boards are in the process of phasing out this type of meter.[7]

Another hazard for old people in the winter months is the possibility of having to face a power-cut, particularly of the electricity supply. Alternative means for heating and cooking should be available. There are a variety of tiny hobs, ovens and grills, using Calor Gas, that are helpful stand-by alternatives.[8]

ACCIDENTAL HYPOTHERMIA

Old people, when living in cold accommodation, are very liable to develop accidental hypothermia during the winter. This refers to a pathological and sometimes fatal lowering of the body temperature.

In a typical situation an old person falls while trying to get out of bed. He then remains on the floor often partly clad, for several hours. Rapid rewarming is dangerous for an old person. The body temperature should be restored naturally and gradually. Hospital treatment is necessary in most cases. Hypothermia is most liable to occur where isolation, unsuitable housing and poor nutrition exist.

Two final points about accidental hypothermia:

(a) Many elderly people do not complain of feeling cold, even when the body temperature is low.

(b) The condition occurs more readily when an old person is on tranquillisers.

Local Old People's Welfare Committees may wish to borrow, for the instruction of its members, the tape recorded talk "Hypothermia in the Elderly". This talk is illustrated with colour transparencies and runs for 25 minutes. Recognition, treatment and prevention are discussed.[9]

A WARM BEDROOM

The heating of an old person's bedroom is just as important as that of the sitting room. In severe weather it may not be possible to keep more than one room warm. It would probably then be preferable to have adequate heat in the living room and have the bed made up in it.

Keeping warm in bed at night can be a problem. A hot water bottle usually helps. Make sure that it has a cover. This will prevent accidental burns. If the old person has a problem with cold feet, it is usually wiser to apply the hot water bottle to the body and not the feet. Also, the wearing of a pair of socks—even two pairs—can help an old person to remain warm in bed.

ELECTRIC BLANKETS

Electric blankets, especially washable ones, are a great comfort to elderly and bedridden people. *Overblankets* are particularly suitable as they have thermostatic temperature control and can be safely left on all night. Pre-heating *underblankets* warm the bed and must be switched off before the person gets into bed (and the plug removed).

The firm, Dreamland's Group Sales, in conjunction with the National Institute of Medical Research, is looking at the problem of hypothermia. To this end, they have designed a low voltage and low wattage electric underblanket. This underblanket is an exception to the general rule and can be used for 24 hours a day. These blankets have a life expectancy of five years. At the moment they can only be hired through the local authorities.[10]

Remind any old person you are helping of the following:

A hot water bottle should never be used with either form of electric blanket.

An electric blanket should never be covered with a rubber sheet, as this would make it overheat.

An electric blanket should never be used for drying out a wet bed.

SOLAR HEATING

In years to come it will be an everyday occurrence for people to rely on the use of the solar heating instead of the conventional fuels we are familar with today. Some scientists are working on this already. An aluminium foil reflector screen, which can be used in conjunction with an electric fire, has recently been patented. The reflector screen costs very little and adds substantially to the heat value of the electric fire.[11]

KITCHEN

Working in the kitchen can become rather strenuous and even hazardous for an old person. I think it is helpful to include here some practical comments that are not mentioned in other sections.

REFRIGERATOR

In a recent survey, it was shown that only approximately 12% of old age pensioners possessed a refrigerator. This number is likely to increase. Refrigerated storage makes a significant contribution both to the independence and nutrition of a housebound person. By prolonging the time perishable food can be kept, the refrigerator and food freezer reduce the number of shopping trips necessary. With a refrigerator, a supply of perishable foods, such as milk and eggs, can always be at hand for simple meals. A good tip regarding the use of a refrigerator for storing food is the following. After using a joint of meat, wrap the remainder in the tin-foil—this helps to preserve the taste and texture of the meat.

It is often easier for an elderly person if the fridge is placed on a small platform above the floor. It would of course be important to make sure that both the platform and the refrigerator are fixed securely.

A well organised kitchen

ELECTRIC KETTLE

An electric kettle is a piece of kitchen equipment that ideally every old person should have. An electric kettle with an automatic cut-out switch (a so called "steamstat") is a good buy. Such a kettle is safer than the conventional one—it prevents the kitchen becoming full of steam and the kettle going dry. This type of kettle is also economic.[12]

An electric kettle can be used anywhere in the house provided there are suitable sockets. This means that during the night, or at times of illness, the electric kettle can be used in the bedroom for the preparation of a hot drink. By making use of coffee bags, tea bags, packet soups, meat extracts and stock cubes, such drinks can be ready within a short time.

Some old people may be rather wary of using an electric kettle. It might be helpful for instructions to be written out, especially if there is some forgetfulness present.[13]

GADGETS

For an old person with disabilities of a physical nature there are several technical problems to be overcome in the kitchen. Taps, for example, may be difficult to turn on and off. Gadgets with long handles are available for this. Tins of food may be difficult to open. An old person with arthritis may find it difficult to operate a conventional tin opener. There are tin openers available which overcome this sort of problem.[14]

A split-level modern cooker is often more convenient for an old person by eliminating the need to bend down to get something hot from the oven. The chances of burns occurring are also reduced.

A spin-dryer helps to make washing lighter to handle and to hang on the clothes line.

PREPARING FOOD

Now a few words about the preparation of food. It is sensible when an old person is cooking potatoes or other vegetables for a pan with a wire container (similar to a chip pan) to be used. This allows the cooked vegetables to be lifted without the necessity of pouring them. A toothed guard fixed onto the side of the cooker will hold a pan handle firmly. The pan can then be stirred with one hand, allowing the other to hold onto a rail or a stick. When an old person suffers from shakiness, for whatever reason, frying as a cooking procedure can be particularly dangerous. Such a person should be encouraged to use grilling as an alternative method of cooking.

PROBLEMS WITH EATING

There are some disabilities, for example, a stroke, that cause particular difficulties in eating. The Nelson knife, which is a special combined knife-fork could be tried. Some older people find it easier to use cutlery that is lighter than the conventional ones. Perspex cutlery, available in chain stores, would be ideal in such circumstances. There are tilting teapot stands available. These allow tea to be poured safely and easily.

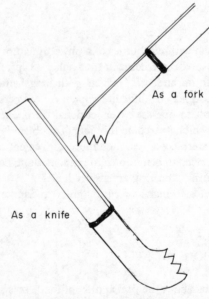

As a fork

As a knife

The Nelson knife

The Disabled Living Foundation Aids Centre will gladly send details of those firms specialising in equipment for the disabled on request. The Foundation would also give information on any aspect of equipment and aids for the disabled.[15]

BATHROOM

Many old people in Britain continue to live in houses where the washing and sanitary facilities are far from ideal. Old age pensioners all too often live in homes with no running hot water. In addition the lavatory accommodation may be outside the house.

For old people with stiff hips it may be sometimes helpful to have the toilet seat raised. A rail fixed to the wall beside the toilet helps such old people in rising.

BATHING AIDS

For many old people, getting in and out of a bath is not only difficult and strenuous, but is also an ordeal. Fortunately a wide variety of aids are now available to ease the situation. These bathing aids assist, not only the handicapped person, but also anyone who is providing assistance.

One of the main essentials is a hand rail attached to the wall. This could be three feet long and situated four or six inches above the edge of the bath. A non-slip bath mat placed at the bottom of the bath is worth considering for many older people. The rubber mat adheres to the bottom of the bath by means of suction cups—these have to be pressed down well on to a wet surface in order that they stick. In addition it is often helpful to fit a bath-board, across the top of the bath, making a kind of shelf for the old person to sit on. This board has to be sufficiently wide so that it will not tilt when sat on. A wooden stool placed alongside the bath (its flat top approximately one inch higher than the bath) is another aid. This enables an elderly person to ease himself gently into the bath. Finally, in some cases one should recommend the use of a bath seat. This would fit inside the bath, about nine inches from the bottom.[16]

Where an old person has a disability which prevents him from sitting in the bath, bathing can be a real problem. Fitting a hand-held spray to the taps is one simple solution. It's cheaper than a shower and is more easily regulated.

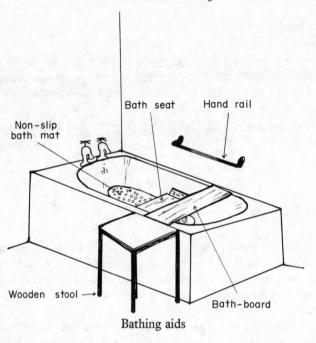

Non-slip bath mat

Bath seat   Hand rail

Wooden stool →

Bath-board

Bathing aids

BEDROOM

THE BED

The weight of the average number of blankets on a bed is 15 lb. Continental down-filled quilts are an excellent way of combining maximum warmth with minimum weight. The use of a Continental quilt reduces the effort of bed making. Terylene filled quilts are now available that can be easily washed.

It should be remembered that sheets made of a cotton and Terylene mixture feel like traditional cotton. They are also light, easy to launder and need no ironing.

A divan bed is possibly the best type of bed for an elderly person who is moderately fit. It is usually possible for an old person to get in and out of a divan bed unaided. It is also easier for such a bed to be made up.

An older person's liability to falls is referred to in more detail on page 50. Care should be taken to ensure that the carpeting in the bedroom is safe. Loose mats on linoleum are particularly likely to cause accidents, but if your friend is reluctant to discard them they can be made safer by a special adhesive tape which attaches to the reverse side.

CONFINED TO BED

Some old people, as a result of physical disability, have to spend many hours each day in bed. In such a situation several other aspects have to be considered. We shall look at these now.

The choice of bedroom is a fundamental issue. In some circumstances, of course, it will not be possible to consider alternatives. Generally speaking, in a two-storey house, it is preferable for the old person's bedroom to be downstairs. Relatives, responsible for carrying trays and such like, will appreciate not having to climb stairs. The choice of bedroom should also be determined to some extent by the sort of view available from the window.

View from the bedroom window is important

Where an elderly person is confined to bed for most of the time, it is better to use a bed of traditional type as opposed to a divan. The extra height of the traditional bed makes for easier nursing. When a person has to use urinals and bedpans in bed, a draw machintosh should be provided. This is a rubber sheet stretched across the bed where there could be soiling. Rubber sheets may be bought from any chemist. As an alternative, a very large polythene bag can be used. It would first have to be split up both sides.

The draw mackintosh is covered with a draw sheet. This can be made by splitting an old sheet lengthwise. Sheets made of flanellette are ideal, as they do not wrinkle when placed on a bed. The sheets should be long enough to enable them to be well tucked in at both sides of the bed. The district nurse would willingly demonstrate the best way of changing a draw sheet without disturbing the bed occupant too much.

COMFORT IN BED

A bed-rest placed at the head of the bed helps to reduce the number of pillows required when a person is sitting up in bed. Some elderly people experience difficulty in moving from a lying down to a sitting up position. A scarf or bandage tied to the head of the bed may be sufficient to overcome the problem. Where disability is pronounced, it may be necessary to use a bed that has a pole at the bed head. Hanging from the top of the pole would be a "monkey-grip" handle, which enables a bedridden person to manoeuvre himself in bed.

Invalids may find the weight of the bedclothes excessive. The use of Continental quilts, referred to earlier, may get over this difficulty. Also, a bed cradle placed over the legs is a solution worth considering in some cases.

What about the meal trays, books, wireless, newspapers and such like, that are essential to the daily life of a bedridden elderly person? A sensibly chosen bed-table is the way to cope with this. Those bed-tables that stand at one side of the bed and that can be swung over are unsatisfactory as they are easily tipped over. The type that fits right across the bed with legs, on castors, on either side is much the best.

Where a double bed is in use, the bed-table would have to be made-to-measure. This could be easily assembled by any handyman in the family and need not be expensive.

COMMODE

A commode would be essential if the elderly person was unable to visit the toilet. It is also a considerable help at night. Various designs are available. Those with back and arm rests are most comfortable and give a lot of support.[17]

BEDPANS AND URINALS

Bedpans and urinals can be bought from your chemist. The polythene bedpans are both less expensive and more comfortable than the stainless steel ones. Urinals are available made out of either glass or polythene. "Female" urinals are easy to use and save the helper's back where the elderly person is rather heavy. These urinals, if not obtainable from the local chemists, may be ordered from any surgical supplies shop.

PREVENTING BEDSORES

When anyone is confined to bed for long periods of time, there is a danger that bedsores will develop. These occur particularly at the foot of the spine and on the heels. It is the prolonged periods of relative immobility that are responsible for bedsores developing. Every effort should be made to prevent this happening, especially as bedsores can take up to three months to heal.

Regular washing of the susceptible areas helps to keep the skin healthy. In addition, vigorous rubbing in of a zinc oxide ointment containing cod liver oil, such as "Thovaline", is a useful measure.

Sheepskins also give good protection against bedsores. They are quite soft and so very comfortable to sit on. Boots made out of sheepskin are available to prevent sores on heels. Sheepskins can be purchased from a surgical supplies shop. Although they are rather costly, it is always preferable to buy a real sheepskin rather than a synthetic one. This is because it is the oil in the natural wool that protects the skin. Do not forget that sheepskins can be laundered in any washing machine. They should be hung outside to dry.

If an old person becomes temporarily very ill, he may need to be nursed lying flat. He would have to be turned from one side to the other every two to four hours to prevent the formation of bedsores. In this type of situation mechanical aids can be used to undertake the work of bedsore prevention. The Hawksley Rippling Bed is such an aid and consists of an air mattress and a small pump that provides air to the mattress. First some parts of the mattress are blown up for four minutes and then the other parts for the next four minutes and so on. The pump is plugged into the household electricity supply. The running costs are minimal. Some local authorities might be prepared to meet the cost of hiring in certain cases.[18]

A full discussion of the problems resulting from loss of control of bladder and bowel will be found on page 82.

LOANING EQUIPMENT

Much of the equipment mentioned here can be loaned either from the local authority or the Red Cross. This even includes such items as commodes and beds fitted with "monkey-grip" handles. For the severely handicapped person, hoists can be borrowed to help move him from bed to chair and back.[19]

MONEY

We all know the difficulty of making ends meet. This is particularly so for old age pensioners. The elderly citizens of our society are probably still not completely used to the change from £.s.d. to decimal coinage. It will be an even less easy job for old people to accommodate themselves to the effects of continuing inflation on the value of the pound.

SOURCES OF INCOME AFTER RETIREMENT

What are likely to be the main sources of income when an old person retires? They are the following:

(a) Income from savings and private investment.
(b) Pension from an employer's superannuation scheme.
(c) Any pension from private insurance.
(d) National insurance retirement pension.
(e) Additional payments and supplementary pensions from the Department of Health and Social Security.
(f) Any grant or allowance from a benevolent fund or charity (your local authority should be aware of such local charities).

It is, of course, evident that many of the problems of the elderly would be alleviated if retirement pensions were related to the cost of living. This must await a change in legislation.

SOCIAL SECURITY

Quite often old people will be entitled to extra financial benefits from the Department of Health and Social Security. Pensioners may be unaware of these. They can claim for help with payment of the rental of a telephone if they are housebound. In such circumstances some social security departments will also meet some of the cost of rental of a television set and the annual licence.

There are one or two publications available which enable members of the public to ensure that they are receiving their full entitlements from the State.[20]

WORKING PENSIONERS

Old age pensioners who are under 70 are allowed to earn so much money per week before their pensions are affected. The regulations regarding the sum that can be earned in this way change from time to time.[21] Earnings do not affect the amount of the pension after the age of 70.

POSSIBLE CLAIMS

Pensioners, even when not housebound, can often receive financial help with house repairs and decorating and even with the payment of rates and rent. Old people, like those of younger years, have their pride. They like to be financially independent of their own family. It is therefore crucial that they are made aware of the financial benefits to which they are entitled. The social security department will be only too pleased to help with this sort of problem.

Certain elderly people will be on special diets, on medical advice, as a result of some illness, e.g. diabetes. Such diets are often expensive. Again financial help may be available for the purchase of food for these special diets. Prescriptions for medicines are of course free for pensioners.

In some instances the old person realises a claim could be made but he is deterred from doing so because of a misguided idea about "not receiving charity". It is basically the job of the social worker to ensure that pensioners receive all their financial entitlements. At times claims may not appear to be receiving the prompt attention they merit. In such circumstances the visitor could perhaps try acting as a catalyst by writing a polite letter or even phoning the social security office.

Where the pensioner is unable to leave his or her home because of physical disability it should be ensured that arrangements have been made for some trustworthy friend or relative to collect the pension on his behalf.

Where an old person is so severely handicapped, either physically or mentally, that he requires constant or repeated attention, an attendance allowance may be claimed from the local social security office.

BANKING FACILITIES

Your local bank manager, a very valuable member of the local community, will be prepared to give advice on budgeting and saving. The range of facilities that the bank provide is not sufficiently appreciated. Some of these are listed here:

(a) Advice on the need to change savings patterns can be given. It is important to ensure that money is soundly invested.

(b) It is possible for stocks and shares to be transferred into a bank's name. This means that any correspondence will be dealt with by that bank.

(c) A customer's Will may be kept in safe keeping at the bank.

(d) Any valuables possessed by the old person could be left in the bank's strong room.

(e) It is possible to make arrangements for rates and other financial commitments to be paid monthly by standing orders. This can save an old person a lot of worry and inconvenience.

(f) In the event of temporary incapacity it is quite easy to arrange for a Mandate authorising a friend or relative to sign cheques. If the incapacity is permanent it might be sensible to arrange for a joint (so called "either or survivor") account. Such a joint account could be conveniently operated by a husband and wife or a mother and daughter. In some cases an old person may wish to delegate entirely the responsibility of handling financial affairs to someone else. This could entail giving someone, usually a solicitor or relative, "Power of Attorney". This type of contract may be terminated at any time by either party provided the old person compensates the person involved for any trouble and expenses involved.

INABILITY TO COPE

An old person may become unable to manage his own affairs by virtue of a psychiatric illness, such as senility (otherwise known as dementia). This means that some disinterested person has to be appointed to take over the management of the affairs. For this to happen it is not necessary for the old person to be "certifiably insane". The procedures in England and in Scotland are different.

In England application is made to the Chief Clerk, Court of Protection, Store Street, London, WC1 7BP. The court requires a certificate or affidavit from the family doctor. This would state that the person concerned was incapable, by reason of mental disorder, of managing or administrating his property and affairs. A receiver, usually a solicitor or an accountant, is appointed to manage the patient's affairs.

In Scotland a *curator bonis* or judicial factor is appointed, following a petition to the Junior Lord Ordinary, the Court of Session, High Street, Edinburgh. If the estate does not exceed £100 per annum, application can be made in the Sheriff Court. A solicitor or chartered accountant is usually appointed *curator bonis*. The petition to the court has to be supported by two medical certificates given "on soul and conscience" that the person is, as a result of his mental state, unable to manage his own affairs or unable to give instructions as to the management.

PAPERS IN ORDER

It is usually advisable for personal papers such as the pension book, insurance policies, Post Office or other Savings Bank book, Friendly Society book, birth certificate, marriage certificate, medical card and Will to be kept in one place, preferably in a fire proof box.

CON MEN

Occasionally one reads in the press of situations where an old person has handed over, in good faith, his life savings, to a door-to-door salesman who has made certain promises. In exchange for the surrendered cash the old people expect to receive a "good investment", a "house improvement", an "up-to-date washing machine" or such like. Old people must be warned not to part with money or to sell anything to anyone who comes to the door, unless they are quite sure about them. They can always say something like, "Please call later—my nephew will be here".

I sometimes see patients who have been defrauded in this way. A year or so ago, I was asked to visit two elderly sisters in a state of distress. They had had a series of visits from two "builder's tradesmen" who had promised to undertake some reconstruction work in the house. These two rogues had insisted on an advance payment of £2000. Unfortunately, the two ladies parted with their money and never saw the men again.

Door-step crooks are smooth operators. They will assume any guise— "an official", "a solicitor bringing news of a legacy", "a tradesman"—in order to extract money from innocent victims.[22]

Dealing with con men

To prevent an elderly person from being tricked or robbed in this way, remind him:

(a) To fit a door-chain or a peep-hole (see page 56) as the best front-line defence;

(b) Not to let anyone into the house until he is satisfied as to who they are.

DEBT

We all know the saying "Look after the pennies and the pounds will look after themselves". This can sound a little idealistic these days. Despite the most careful budgeting, many people are quite unable to save. Being in debt can be a most demoralising experience. Where an elderly person has a lot of problems as a result of money worries, it would be appropriate to advise him to seek help from a social worker.[23]

LEGAL MATTERS

MAKING A WILL

It is vitally important for every man and woman to make a Will. After all, everyone has something to bequeath, even if it's only the money in the wallet or purse. Possessions fall into two classes, real property and personal property. Real property consists of freehold estates (which in ordinary cases means the owner's house and the land it stands on). Personal property is every other possession, including personal effects.

There is no fixed form of Will, but the following points should be borne in mind:

(a) The Will must be in writing, i.e. handwriting or typewriting.

(b) If the Will is being made in the testator's own handwriting, it must be dated, and signed at the end in the following manner: "Written by my own hand at (place) on (date)".

(c) If the Will is typewritten or written by someone other than the testator, then the testator must sign at the foot of every page and at the end of the Will in the presence of two witnesses. After his signature, he should write the date. The witnesses do not need to know the contents of the Will but they should not derive any benefit from the Will. The witnesses sign at the end of the Will only, opposite the testator's signature and underneath in each case they must write their occupation and address and add the word "Witness".

(d) The best advice that can be offered to persons wishing to make a Will is to consult a lawyer. By so doing they can be sure that their wishes will be carried out and the lawyer's fees for drawing up a normal type of Will are usually very moderate.

It is often convenient to arrange for a solicitor or the bank to be executor to the Will.

There are important differences in the law regarding the making of a Will in the four parts of the United Kingdom. In certain circumstances a Will, for example, made out according to the English form could be invalid in Scotland and vice versa.

In the event of a death, the deceased's family may find itself short of money for immediate use. Following death bank deposits, shares and resources in other forms of savings are frozen until the Will is proven and probate granted. The operation of a joint account (see previous section) ensures that the survivor has continuing access to money in the bank.

Before any part of an estate is shared out, official permission has to be obtained from a probate registry. Your registrar of births and deaths will give you a leaflet, Form 48, which explains the procedure and also gives the addresses of probate registries. In Scotland, where a Will has been made, "confirmation" must be obtained from the Sheriff Clerk. Where there are any problems, a solicitor should be consulted.

LEGAL AID

Legal aid, either free or at a reduced cost, is available today for those members of the public, whose means are fairly modest. A person's entitlement depends on his income and savings and whether or not he is responsible for dependent children or relatives.

Under the legal aid scheme a solicitor can write letters for the client, prepare documents, help prepare a Will, deal with any hire purchase problems and resolve difficulties between a tenant and a landlord. Anyone can apply for legal aid and a relative or friend may apply on behalf of someone who is incapable of doing so on his own.

The solicitor may even visit an old person in his own house where there is incapacity.[24]

SHOPPERS' RIGHTS

Elderly people may need to be reminded that, as shoppers, they have certain rights. Nobody should be afraid to complain to a shop about goods that are found, after purchase, to be broken or damaged in some way. Politely, but firmly, any unsatisfactory goods, along with the receipt or cheque stub, should be returned to the shop manager.

When the manager is not helpful, it might then be appropriate to write a letter to the managing director at head office. Alternately, contact could be made with the trade association which covers the type of goods you are complaining about. The local library would have the names and addresses of both of these.

If the matter is still not satisfactorily concluded, the firm could be sued for the return of the money or for compensation. Legal advice should be obtained at this stage.

Your local Director of Consumer Protection would always be able to advise you on the sensible approach to adopt with a problem of this kind.

WHEN SOMEONE DIES

MEDICAL CERTIFICATE

You may find yourself responsible for making the necessary arrangements in the event of a death. If the death happens at night and is sudden and unexpected the doctor should be notified at once. Otherwise, the doctor can be called in the morning.

The law requires that every death in this country is registered. It is the deceased's doctor who will normally issue the certificate of cause of death needed by the registrar.

In England and Wales a death has to be reported to the coroner if the deceased had not been seen by the doctor during his last illness. Also, any death that is sudden or the result, directly or indirectly, of an accident has to be reported to the coroner.

In Scotland, where there is any doubt about the cause of death, the matter should be referred to the full-time law officer, known as the procurator fiscal.

THE HOUSE

If you are living in a house that was owned or rented by the deceased, you should clarify your own situation as soon as possible with the landlord (this is the local authority if you are living in a council house) or the building society. It is not wise to move away temporarily without first arranging for the rent payment or the mortgage repayments to continue.[25]

FUNERAL EXPENSES

Some people like to make financial provision for funeral expenses, whether for cremation or burial. Pharos Assurance Friendly Society operates a scheme to which anyone, up to the age of 80 years, may apply to join. The Society is registered in accordance with the various Friendly Societies Acts and has to comply with the terms of such Acts.[26]

CHAPTER 4

Other Ways of Helping

PREVENTING FALLS AND FIRES

It is particularly important to ensure that old people do not stumble and fall in their own homes. Older people are liable to fractures, particularly of the thigh bone, after such falls. Occasionally, of course, falls occur outside the house too. In frosty weather, for example, steps and paths may be very slippery—a little sprinkled salt can be very helpful in preventing accidents.

RISK OF FALLING

Inside the home, falls often occur when an elderly person takes chances, especially when overtired. Standing on a chair and carrying heavy loads are two examples.

Floor coverings are often at fault. Highly polished linoleum should be avoided. Slip-resistant polish, made by the major manufacturers, is available from hardware stores. Water spilt on the floor can lead to trouble. Talcum powder on the bathroom floor is dangerous. Walking about in stocking feet is risky, except in rooms with carpets.

Dark corners when possible, should be well lit. Old rugs or stair carpets can develop holes—traps for unsuspecting feet. In such circumstances the wisest, though not perhaps the most popular thing to do, is to remove the offending rug or carpet altogether. Alternately, non-slip rubber mesh underlay can be placed under a loose mat.

Take care in slippery weather

Badly fitting shoes in themselves can lead to stumbles. A visit to the shoe repairer's, or even the shoe shop, might be encouraged.

Steep stairs, especially those without bannisters, are very liable to result in an old person falling.

FIRE HAZARDS

There are several common sense things that a visitor can attend to in order to reduce the risk of fire in an old person's home. The plug of the television set should be taken out each night and there should be a guard at the coal fire. Electric fires should not be placed in the middle of the room and flexes should be well tucked away from the walls.[1] Fireguards should be used if an open fire is insisted upon, as a safety precaution in case of falls.

Those responsible for old people living at home should pay attention to the following points:

Ensure that all heating appliances are serviced regularly.

See that oil heaters are fixed to the wall or the floor in a safe place.

See that candles and nightlights, if used, are placed in a saucer of water.

Check that the house does not need rewiring.[2]

Make sure that electric power points are not overloaded with too many appliances.

Direct advice could with advantage be given to old people about the more obvious fire risks:

Do not leave chip pans or a frying pan unattended (if there is a fire from these, the heat should be turned off and the pan covered with a lid, metal tray, damp cloth or the type of fire blanket mentioned later).

Do not pour paraffin on a sulky fire or draw it up with a newspaper.

Do not keep a clock on the mantlepicece (clothes can so easily catch alight when the time is being checked).

Do not get into bed with an electric underblanket before the blanket is switched off and the plug removed. (Also never use a hot water bottle along with an electric blanket.)

A fire blanket, neatly folded in a canister fixed on a wall, gives a very simple and efficient protection against fire in a home. It is flame resistant and can be quickly released by pulling on a string protruding from the bottom of the holder. The blanket, once used, can be easily washed.[3]

SMOKERS BEWARE

The heavy smoker puts himself at an increased risk from the point of view of fire. The rule is that people should never smoke in bed. Where an old person persistently ignores this advice enquiries should perhaps be made about the use of fire resistant bedding. It might save someone's life or prevent a disfiguring burn.

LAST LOOK ROUND

It is very easy for a cooker to be left switched on. This is especially so when someone calls. Before you leave after visiting an elderly person make sure that nothing has been left on accidentally. Have a last look round—are any clothes or tea towels hanging too close to a fire or cooker?

MAINTENANCE OF HOUSE AND GARDEN

HELP FROM THE COMMUNITY

Old people, as a result of frailty, may be unable to spring clean their house as often or as thoroughly as before. This in turn can lead to a lot of worry and frustration. The old person then tends to worry about what the neighbours think. In many areas throughout Britain young people are undertaking valuable community work by helping pensioners with decorating. Possibly in the area in which you live there is a school or a Scout Troup or similar youth organisation which would be only too delighted to provide some form of practical help for a particular old person.

A large garden, rich with flowers and fruit trees, can turn from being a source of joy in one's earlier years to being a burden later on. This is again where Scouts and other groups can perform a valuable service by undertaking regular maintenance work in the garden by mowing lawns, clipping hedges and weeding borders.

Some local authorities provide a gardening service. The relevant social services department will provide you with details.

COPING WITH THE GARDEN

However keen a gardener an old person may be, he is usually interested to hear of any labour-saving devices. Specially designed garden tools come into this category.[4]

Getting a local scout troop to help

If you know someone with an area of garden which is too big to manage, here is a splendid idea. Cover the ground with a square shaped section of polythene. On top of this spread a layer of chippings a few inches deep. This will effectively stop the growth of weeds. Small circles of polythene can be cut out at appropriate places and shrubs planted there. Hey presto! an instant and easy to maintain garden.

An elderly person can continue to be interested in gardening without having to go outside his house at all. Window boxes, for example, can be a lively source of interest. Also some vegetables can be grown indoors. I refer to tomatoes, bean sprouts, mustard and cress and even green peppers. These can provide a welcome addition to the kitchen stock.

It is probably sensible to advise any elderly gardener to get rid of any poisonous chemicals that he uses. Older people, as a result of poor memory, may forget to take the usual precautions with these substances, such as wearing gloves or washing hands after use. This can have serious consequences.[5]

KEEPING THE HOUSE IN GOOD ORDER

Old people may be concerned about house repairs that require attention —a leaking roof, a fuse requiring mending, a squeaking door hinge.

Perhaps you know a Do-it-yourself expert? Go ahead and ask him to help, providing the elderly person agrees.

The Housing Act 1974 provides for grants to be made available to owner-occupiers, landlords and tenants in England and Wales for the improvement and repair of sound older houses, usually of the pre-1961 vintage. The equivalent legislation in Scotland provides for the improvement and repair normally of houses that have been built, or converted, before 1964. The grants cover a wide range of work that may be needed to raise the standard of a house or keep it in good repair. The following are examples of situations, where help may be given:

No proper bathroom

No hot and cold water supply

No inside W.C. or kitchen sink

Absence of damp-proof course

An inadequate staircase

Poor lighting or ventilation

Need for thermal insulation

Converting a large house into flats.

In the case of a registered disabled person, an improvement grant may be given for work considered necessary to adapt an existing dwelling to his accommodation and welfare needs.[6]

SECURITY OF THE HOME

On visits to an old person's home we must make sure that there are no open invitations to burglars.

Notes about being "Away till Tuesday" should not be displayed on the front door. Likewise keys should not be hidden under obvious places like door mats or hung with a string behind the letter box.

It is advisable for a light to be left on in the sitting room—with the curtains closed—when the elderly person is out for the evening.

Make sure that jewellery is kept in a safe place. Small wall safes are quite inexpensive (about £10).

The best way to ensure that house is secure is to call at the local police station and ask for the crime prevention officer to call. He will make a security survey of any house and provide a written report free of charge.

A one-way peephole can be fitted into the front door. This enables the householder to see out but not allow the person outside to see in. Thieves tend to make an entrance by the back door. This should then ideally be fitted with a bolt as well as a lock.

Before an old person retires to bed, all downstairs windows, especially those at the back, should be shut and snibbed.

Readers should consult Chapter 6 for a further discussion of this matter.

PETS

COMPANIONSHIP

Most of us know from our childhood days that having a pet is a very rewarding experience.

Companionship of pets . . .

Older people, too, enjoy the company of their pets. A dog or a cat provides companionship, loyalty and fun. Such pets also provide an object upon which an old person can direct a bit of affection and love.

Keeping a pet is a popular pastime in Great Britain. In these isles there is 1 dog to every 9.5 people. In the States the dog-human ratio is even more striking, 1 to 6.

The cost of both purchase and upkeep must be borne in mind when advising an elderly person about a pet. Any dog over the age of six months has to have a licence and this is renewable each year.[7] The National Canine Defence League will pay a pensioner's dog licence in cases of real hardship.[8] Applicants, recommended by a J.P., priest or minister, doctor, vet, D.H.S.S. official or a policeman, must not be able to afford their own T.V. licence!

Many people choose a cat rather than a dog as daily walks are not required.

BOARDING FACILITIES

If an elderly person goes into hospital for a spell, it is, of course, important to ensure that satisfactory boarding arrangements are made for pets. Where finances are tight, the local authority will usually bear the costs of boarding (under Section 48 of the National Assistance Act, 1948). The Royal Society for the Prevention of Cruelty to Animals will advise and help in any situation involving pets. Often the Society will transport the animal to boarding kennels or a cattery on behalf of the local authority.[9]

The Scottish Society for Prevention of Cruelty to Animals provides a similar service north of the border.[10]

In Scotland the Dog Aid Society of Scotland Limited can occasionally help with the boarding of dogs, whose owners live in the immediate area of Edinburgh. The scheme applies only to those people, who are in poor circumstances and who need to undergo hospital treatment.[11]

BUDGIES

A budgerigar in a cage can often make a most welcome addition to an old person's household. Such birds cost no more than one or two pounds and perhaps five or six pence a week to keep. Considering the average lifespan is ten years this is good value for money. If you want a budgie to talk, a young cock or hen between six and nine weeks must be chosen.

Budgies have taken over from dogs and cats in the popularity stakes. This is probably because they are cheerful, decorative pets with a lot of character. Their needs are simple: regular food, water and a clean cage.

If the owner of a budgerigar decides to move into a residential home or a sheltered housing scheme the bird is often permitted to go too.

The Companionship Trust is a charity that exists to provide individual old people, who are lonely or housebound, with a budgerigar, and if needed, a cage. The Trust works closely with social services departments and voluntary organisations, such as Old Peoples' Welfare Committees.[12]

BIRD WATCHING

Many elderly people derive immense satisfaction from the pastime of bird watching. The Royal Society for the Protection of Birds are geared to this aspect of old people's welfare. On receipt of a stamped envelope the Society will send leaflets on the feeding of wild birds and plans for making D.I.Y. nest boxes and bird tables. This garden bird equipment is inexpensive and designed for those with no carpentry skills and few tools.[13]

The book *The New Bird Table* could help an old person to further his interest in this pursuit.[14]

The Wildfowl Trust recently started an intriguing "Adopt a Duck" Scheme. In exchange for a small sum of money, any member of the public is kept informed of the progress of a particular duck that has been examined and ringed for research purposes prior to release. Any older person can in this way continue to have an interest in bird life.[15]

FISH

A pastime that is becoming very popular is fish-keeping. There is no doubt that watching the silent, graceful movements of fish is very relaxing —and quite often better value for money than gazing at the television screen. The local aquarium society would be only too pleased to advise

... even a single goldfish

any pensioner keen to join the ranks of the enthusiasts. Whether it involves a single goldfish in a bowl or several tropical fish in a large heated tank, the hobby involves a lot of fun.[16]

WHAT THE VET CAN DO

When an old person's pet is ill for some reason, you should try and ensure that the animal gets attention from a veterinary surgeon. If the owner is poor, it is probably worth explaining the situation to the vet. He will generally be very helpful and understanding. In your area there may exist a People's Dispensary for Sick Animals.

Some old people, because of physical disability, such as rheumatism, may have difficulty in regularly grooming their dogs, especially if these are of the shaggy or long-haired variety. This is something a regular

visitor could undertake. In addition it might be beneficial for the pet to
be taken to the vet three or four times a year for a check-up. Matted hair
could be dealt with and also the general condition observed. After all,
as with humans, prevention is better than cure.

THE DEATH OF A PET

The death of a favourite pet can be a catastrophic experience for an old
person. This will be especially so where the pet has been a real companion.
You should be prepared to provide a shoulder to weep on. Support at
such a time may be critical even to the extent of preventing admission to
a psychiatric hospital.

TRANSPORT

THE ELDERLY DRIVER

Many people approaching retirement have to make a fundamental
decision about the family car. To sell or not to sell. Two factors are
crucial in this. These are the cost of keeping the car on the road and the
person's state of health.

Where health is impaired to any degree the decision is an easy one.
In fact, for many it is a distinct relief not to have to face the stress of
driving a car any more.

In January 1976 new regulations regarding the granting of driving
licenses came into force. Driving licences are now valid until the holders'
70th birthday, with the following exceptions. Any person suffering from
certain disabilities will be given a licence for a period of one, two or three
years. Similarly, drivers over the age of 70 will have their licences renewed
for one, two or three years, depending on the recommendation made by
the examining doctor. A leaflet explaining these regulations can be
obtained from the Post Office.

The disabled driver who is about to retire has particular problems.

Transport is a lifeline

The Disabled Drivers' Association will give a lot of support and practical advice to such a person.[17]

As has been mentioned before, transport represents a type of lifeline for the elderly. Fortunately the public is now aware of this. Organisations such as the W.R.V.S. and the Red Cross often provide a Community Car Service. This enables the elderly and disabled to visit relatives and close friends in hospital, and also to visit the dentist and chiropodist.

GOING BY BUS

The new style pay-as-you-enter bus can be a source of worry to old people. After all, it takes some time to get used to the idea of carrying loose change with you for such bus journeys. The public tends to forget

Going by bus

that old people, because of their diminished agility, often need that extra moment or so to climb onto the platform of a bus. Some say that when an elderly person carries a stick this automatically leads the conductor, and the other passengers, to being more considerate.

Many local authorities provide concessionary bus fares for pensioners. In some areas they are even allowed to travel on buses free—within stated times.

SHOPPING

Old people rely heavily on the resources of the local shops. Often transport is needed so that this important contact can be continued. Naturally pensioners prefer to avoid the rush hour periods. Also, they can find supermarkets somewhat daunting. A little gentle, but tactful guidance is often appreciated in these places.

May I insert here a personal observation? So few shops nowadays seem to have chairs for the elderly and also disabled people to sit down on. What about starting a campaign about this in your own locality?

THE RAILWAYS

British Rail have several concessions of which pensioners should be aware. Your local station will provide details of these schemes such as the "Senior Citizens' Railcard", the purchase of which enables one to travel for half price on certain routes.

If you are arranging for an elderly relative who is chairbound to travel by train, possible difficulties should first be discussed with an official at the station. Sometimes wheel chairs can be borrowed from the Red Cross or the local authorities for such a journey.

GETTING ADVICE

If you wish expert advice on a transport problem concerned with the elderly, you should contact Age Concern[18] or your local Old Peoples' Welfare Committee.

GETTING PROFESSIONAL HELP

When in doubt about an old person's condition never hesitate to seek professional advice. The family doctor is, of course, the key person here. Help should also be sought in appropriate circumstances from the minister or priest, the health visitor, the district nurse and the social services department.

CHAPTER 5

Health

Positive thinking is needed here. Unfortunately many of the public still feel that little can be done for an elderly man or woman who is ill—it is assumed that the old person's condition is simply due to his age. In fact, most old people, who are unwell, are suffering from a treatable disease of one sort or another.[1]

It is important to encourage the elderly themselves to look after their health properly. Consulting the doctor when a symptom first appears, rather than waiting until a disease process is well advanced, makes sense. Prevention and early treatment are the keynotes.

TAKING MEDICINES

Many old people are on a variety of pills and tonics. Some may be on as many as twelve different medicines a day. This can be very perplexing for an elderly person. In such circumstances it might be helpful to label empty matchboxes with the times throughout the day at which tablets were to be taken, e.g. breakfast, lunch, teatime, and bedtime. Each evening the old person could then fill the matchboxes with the correct number of tablets for the next day. I am sure this would be worth trying in some cases.

If you see any unused but half empty medicine bottles in a house you should tactfully advise the old person to flush the pills and medicines down the lavatory or to return them to the chemist. When in doubt the district nurse should be consulted on these points.

People who are on certain drugs (e.g. cortico-steroids and anticoagulants) are often given a card to carry indicating which drug they are on. Such a card could even be fixed on the clothing. In the event of a medical emergency the attending doctor would then be aware of this important fact.

Prescriptions are now available free for women over 60 and men over 65. The relevant section on the back of the prescription is completed by the old person or a friend who is acting on his behalf.

SHOPLIFTING

Self-service stores, and supermarkets in particular, can be rather daunting places for an older person to shop in. Where an element of

Supermarkets can be daunting places

absent-mindedness exists, there is a real risk that, as a result of a genuine mistake, goods will be taken and not paid for.

Confusion, resulting in an act of absent-minded shoplifting, occurs especially when an elderly person has any pressing worries. It also tends to happen when certain types of drugs are prescribed by the doctor. Tranquillisers, antidepressants and those for high blood pressure are most often to blame in this respect.

It is very difficult to prove innocence, once a charge of shoplifting is made. The elderly and their relatives should be aware of this and see that extra care is taken on those supermarket shopping sprees.

CHILDREN AND DRUG POISONING

In recent years several youngsters have tragically died following accidental poisoning from medicines that looked like sweets. Any old person living with grandchildren has a responsibility to see that any drugs being taken are out of reach of toddlers.

The Health Departments in Britain have been concerned about this problem. It has now been officially recommended that certain tablets after 1976 will be dispensed only in special opaque or dark tinted packs. Some elderly people will have difficulty in dealing with this new packaging, as a result of arthritis and such like. In these cases conventional containers would still be supplied.

SLEEP

A number of old people have difficulty with their sleep. We should remember, however, that generally speaking elderly people require less sleep than those of middle years or younger. Five or six hours sleep in an old person is usually quite sufficient. As people age they find they get off to sleep less easily. Also, sleep tends to become more broken. An elderly person should be reassured that it is natural to have short spells lying awake at night and that this does not damage health.

Old people should be advised to adapt a relaxing pottering routine

Insomnia

during the half-hour before bed-time. Watching a gripping horror film on television is not the best approach to this! At times insomnia can result from a medical condition, such as arthritis. Here the family doctor would prescribe appropriate pills.

For a lot of people the taking of a milk beverage last thing at night helps to promote good sleep. Tea and coffee should be avoided late at night. They both contain caffeine, which stimulates the brain.

Alcohol in the form of whisky or brandy is often a valuable and effective night-cap. Sleeping pills, or any other form of tablet, must never be taken with alcohol.

Where an old person is taking sleeping tablets every night there are two points to bear in mind. First, if at all possible, the bottle of sleeping tablets should be in a place other than on the bedside table. Where the supply is beside the bed, there is a serious risk that the old person may wake up in the middle of the night and inadvertently repeat the dose. Secondly, an old person may react badly to a particular type of sleeping tablet.

Barbiturates, until quite recently, were the most regularly prescribed form of sleeping tablet. Quite often, however, an old person taking barbiturates last thing at night experiences confusion on waking the next day. This can last for as long as two to three hours. New types of sleeping tablets are now available that avoid this complication.[2]

SEX

The myths regarding sexuality and elderly people are worth exploring. Unfortunately there is room for enlightenment so far as public attitudes are concerned. To a great degree, the taboos regarding sex in adolescence and adulthood have been laid aside. By contrast, many still feel that sexual desire and sexual activity cease, or should cease, in old age.

The scientific knowledge that has been accumulated in recent years indicates that the reverse is true. In a large number of men and women over 60 years of age, sexual feelings continue to exist.

Both the elderly themselves and the community at large need to be reassured that to have sexual desires after middle age is not unusual or abnormal or immoral. A greater awareness of this will prevent some of the unintentional cruelty experienced by old people. An aged couple living for example with their children or in a residential home are too often denied the privacy that is their right. Elderly widows or widowers, interested in re-marriage, should not be put off by "friends" trying to persuade them "not to make fools of themselves".

EYES, EARS, TEETH AND FEET

Unfortunately people don't realise how important and vital all these are. We seem to take their efficiency for granted and so feel resentful when things go wrong. Old people can continue to have good eyesight, efficient hearing, properly fitting dentures and healthy feet—well into retirement—providing a sensible attitude prevails.

SPECTACLES

Most people, as they grow older, require glasses for reading. Elderly people should have their eyes tested by their family doctor every two years or so. Any sudden deterioration in eyesight must be reported to the doctor at once.

If there was thought to be any serious abnormality or disease of the eyes, the doctor would arrange for the old person to see a specialist. In certain circumstances this examination could be done at home.

Where there is a need for spectacles, the doctor would advise referral to one of the three types of highly qualified people working in the general ophthalmic services: an ophthalmic medical practitioner, who is a doctor who tests sight and prescribes glasses, an ophthalmic optician, who is not medically qualified but who tests sight and prescribes glasses and also supplies glasses, or a dispensing optician who simply provides glasses for a prescription.

Spectacles that get broken should be returned to the optician who has provided them. Any optician, however, undertaking National Health Service work would usually agree to mend them.

Some elderly people may not be able to afford the cost of new spectacles or that of repairing spectacles. The optician will supply a form of application (Form F.1), which has to be submitted to the Department of Health and Social Security.

READING AIDS

When an old person has difficulty in reading, there are two simple remedies that are worth considering:

(a) Does the reading lamp need a stronger electric bulb? A tremendous difference results when a bulb of 60 watt is replaced by one of 200 watt. Such a manoeuvre may enable an elderly person to read small print again.

(b) Would a magnifying glass be helpful? Both the Disabled Living Foundation and the Scottish Information Service for the Disabled will give full information on the available range of magnifiers and also prismatic recumbent spectacles for use by the bedridden when reading or watching television.[3]

THE BLIND AND THE PARTIALLY SIGHTED

It is essential for any blind or partially sighted person to be treated as normally as possible. Don't talk down to blind people. Also avoid smothering the blind with kindness and pity.

When talking to the blind, we should use normal words and normal tones.

What blind people greatly appreciate is someone providing a running commentary on what's going on. This would apply when a helper is sitting sharing a television programme or going for a walk.

The Royal National Institute for the Blind will gladly supply any relevant information to the blind and also their relatives.[4] The Institute provides talking books for the blind. For an elderly blind person the choice of a suitable talking book must be given careful consideration. As memory and concentration may be impaired books for teenagers might be more appropriate than some more sophisticated material.

BLIND AIDS

The blind aids that are in use today have been made primarily to ensure a blind person's safety. This applies to the conventional short white stick and the more recently introduced long white stick. Guide dogs are owned by only about 2% of blind people. This is because of the stringent requirements laid down by the Guide Dogs for the Blind Association.[5]

A few years ago sonar torches came on the market. These emit a high-pitched tone which changes its quality when reflected back from an obstacle. Unfortunately the first sonar devices were too complicated to use and never became popular.

A Nottingham Obstacle Detector (N.O.D.) has recently been produced. This is carried in the pocket and only reflects from obstacles within eight feet. It is intended mainly for use along with either a white stick or dog. There seems to be a place for it also as an aid indoors.[6]

The B.B.C. has published a comprehensive guide, *In Touch—aids and services for blind and partially sighted people*. This is of particular value to the relatives of the blind.[7]

HEARING AIDS

Hearing, just like eyesight, can deteriorate almost imperceptibly in an old person.

Deafness can be an exasperating experience for the sufferer and almost as much for the person who is trying to communicate. Many deaf old people experience serious social isolation. Arrangements should therefore be made for a hearing aid to be fitted at an early stage, if medically indicated.

For many years "Medescro", body-worn, hearing aids have been obtainable free of charge under the National Health Service.

Since 1974 the more convenient behind-the-ear hearing aids have been also available. These are thought to be suitable for the majority of people with impaired hearing. At the moment this new type of hearing aid is being prescribed for certain priority groups in the population. These include war pensioners, people of any age in full-time or part-time employment and any person with an exceptional medical need. It is hoped within a few years that everyone needing a behind-the-ear hearing aid will be supplied with one.

The family doctor can arrange for a person with defective hearing to see an ear, nose and throat specialist. If a hearing aid is thought to be necessary, referral would then be made to a Hearing Aid Distribution Centre. The Centre provides replacement batteries and a repair service free.

Habitual users of hearing aids should have a periodic medical examination to ensure that wax is not impacted in the external ear canal. This can result from frequent insertion of the ear piece. The hearing aid itself should be serviced regularly. Most faults that do arise are easily remedied. An audible feed-back squeal may be simply due to poor fitting of the aid, and crackling or intermittent non-function can often be corrected by replacing a worn flex.[8]

Some people for personal reasons prefer to buy a commercially marketed hearing aid. In these circumstances it is advisable to apply to the Royal National Institute for the Deaf for their booklet *Hearing Aids*.[9]

There has recently been an interesting development in the hearing aid field. Portable communicators have been designed to aid person-to-person communication. These aids are particularly of value in a hospital or a home for the elderly. By means of such an instrument a very deaf old person can have a normal private conversation with a relative or doctor.[10]

ORGANISATIONS FOR THE DEAF

The Royal National Institute for the Deaf provides free advice on welfare, housing and hearing loss problems. The Institute will also provide details of the special door bells, flashing lights and louder telephones which are available to help the deaf. It publishes the magazine *Hearing*.[11]

The British Association of the Hard of Hearing exists to foster the social and cultural activities for those who become wholly or partially deaf. It publishes a quarterly magazine *Hark!* Several most helpful leaflets are produced. In one of these *Other Aids to Hearing*, the use of hearing aid adaptors is described, whereby a deaf person can hear a radio or a television without having to turn up the volume to a disastrous level.[12]

CARE OF THE TEETH

One of the most important things is to ensure that as people become older their dental condition is maintained and is not allowed to deteriorate. It is preferable for major dental changes not to be undertaken in older people if at all possible. These include the renewal of several teeth and the provision of dentures where none had been worn previously.

The ideal thing is for a person to retain their natural teeth throughout life. In an older person it is not essential for him to have a full complement of natural teeth. If there are sufficient back teeth for chewing and an adequate number of front ones for appearance partial dentures may not be necessary—indeed sometimes they are inadvisable. Your dentist will give you advice.

The use of a medium/hard short-head toothbrush is recommended after each meal. Where partial dentures are worn, these must be removed after each meal and also scrubbed with a brush. To avoid any breakages, they should be washed over a basin full of water. Partial dentures should not be worn at night. If an older person finds difficulty in holding the handle of a toothbrush, this can be modified by putting over the handle a bicycle grip or some similar sleeve which increases the handle diameter.

At times you may find yourself responsible for cleaning an old person's teeth. The secret is to brush from the gums towards the teeth, not from side to side. Don't forget the backs as well as the sides of them.

DENTURES

If the natural teeth cannot be saved (and 80% of the British adult population over 55 are without any natural teeth), then dentures should be provided before the old person becomes too advanced in years. Learning to cope with dentures would then be difficult and, in some cases, impossible. After the provision of dentures, dental supervision continues to be essential. There is an unfortunate tendency to think thatdentures, once provided, are everlasting. This is not so and many old people drift into the seventies and eighties with poor dentures. The older person's more limited capacity for adaptation may make it very difficult for new and well fitting dentures to be accepted.

EATING PROBLEMS

Many elderly people experience difficulty in chewing food. This might be because of the poor condition of the natural teeth or because of ill fitting dentures. It is quite possible for food to be prepared in a liquidiser or a mincer. But this can result in a rather monotonous texture of diet.

Those who cannot chew properly tend to limit themselves to sweet, easily managed foodstuffs, usually carbohydrates such as bread, pastry, potatoes and jam. This often results in an imperfect diet being taken. Whilst such people are not unwell, they are not as healthy as they might be.

There are some people who, due to the condition of the gums under their dentures, experience difficulty and pain on biting as well as in chewing. In such circumstances people should not attempt to bite off food or to chew vigorously. The food should be cut up well or minced before it is put in the mouth.

We can see that dentures and natural teeth help an old person to select a more interesting and varied diet. Also, and most significantly, they contribute considerably towards a person's morale by maintaining his facial appearance. On the other hand, ageing of the face tends to be obvious in the old person who does not wear dentures.

REGULAR VISITS TO THE DENTIST

Old people with natural teeth should visit their dentist every year, while those with no natural teeth should visit their dentist at least once every five years. In the case of dentures, this does not mean that replacement dentures are necessary every five years. Frequently a minor adjustment to the dentures is sufficient to maintain good oral hygiene. Neglect, on the other hand, will rapidly lead to deterioration.

Ideally, then, all elderly people should receive regular dental treatment. Occasionally, as in circumstances of reduced mobility, a domiciliary visit is necessary. Under the National Health Service, a dentist is able to make such a visit and the fee is relatively small. The facilities, however, for giving home treatment are rather limited. To undertake all but the simplest treatments in dentistry, a dental surgery is almost essential. It is, therefore, most important that before an old person becomes housebound his dental condition is reviewed and restored to some degree of function if at all possible. In some areas, day hospitals provide facilities for the assessment of the dental condition of older people and for treatment. If an old person is admitted to hospital, his dentures should be marked by the dentist. This is to ensure that there is no mixing up of dentures, which often, to nursing staff, look identical.

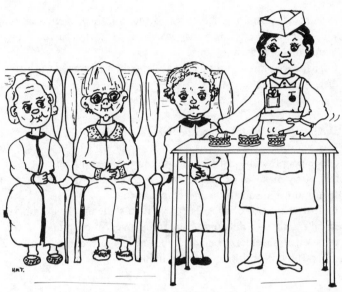

Dentures all look identical

FOOT CARE

The importance of old people remaining mobile has been stressed
earlier. This in part depends on their adopting a sensible attitude to their
feet. There will be fewer falls if shoes are worn in preference to slippers.
When slippers are worn, they should be a comfortable fit. Foot comfort
can be further enhanced by the avoidance of restrictive garments round
the legs. Neither wearing tight underwear, nor using gnarled old bits of
elastic instead of garters, helps in this respect.

A regular visit to a chiropodist can be a morale booster for an older
person by helping to keep his feet in good trim. In most places a chiropody
service is available for elderly people and is provided by the local authority
or one of the voluntary bodies. If the old person is housebound, arrangements can often be made for the chiropodist to pay a home visit. The
Society of Chiropodists will supply the names and addresses of chiropodists
in private practice. The Institute of Chiropodists has a comprehensive
list of chiropodists as well.[13]

A word of warning. Diabetics and those with poor circulation should never attempt to cut their own toe nails. Injuries to toes can lead to infection or other serious consequences.

Corns, hard skin and difficult nails should all be dealt with by a chiropodist.

RECOVERY FROM A STROKE

Older people may experience disability as a result of a stroke. Fortunately many make an excellent recovery from this. In fact a large number return to normal social life and employment.

During the acute phase of a stroke illness the emphasis is naturally on medical treatment. This may have to be given in hospital.

It is when an elderly person is beginning to recuperate after a stroke that a variety of problems come to light.

THE HANDICAPS

A person who has had a stroke realises that he is unable to do a lot of things previously tackled almost without thinking. Weakness can persist for some time in the leg, and especially the hand, on the side of the body affected by the stroke. These handicaps in turn mean that assistance is required with dressing, standing and walking.

Ideally exercises should be undertaken regularly under the guidance of a physiotherapist. Where this does not happen, the affected arm and leg have less chance of recovering their full function.

Even more frustrating than these problems are the occasions where the ability to speak, and also to understand the speech of others, is affected. Essentially this means that messages can neither be given nor received by the person affected.

STROKE PATIENTS' DISTRESS

It is inevitable that faced with these disabilities the person recovering from a stroke tends to be emotional at times. He is afraid of ridicule and experiences a lack of confidence. There are moments of despair.

The stroke patient may even turn his anger, and frustration onto his family. A devoted wife, for example, may be subject to unexpected abuse and foul language. It is as if the disabled person temporarily finds relief in blaming someone else for the handicap.

SUPPORT FOR THE FAMILY

The families of stroke patients need a lot of support. Friends may, however, find it difficult to visit because of inability to face the unusual. This can lead to the family concerned feeling very isolated.

The Chest and Heart Association publishes books and leaflets which give patients and their families information and fuller understanding of strokes.[14]

REHABILITATION

While a person is recovering from a stroke the family doctor, the district nurse and perhaps also the hospital specialist will continue to give advice to the patient and his family. Of equal importance is the contribution that can be made by experts in rehabilitation. Later on (page 94) I stress how physiotherapists, occupational therapists, speech therapists and dieticians are more and more involved in helping old people in their own homes.

The improvement brought about by these members of the rehabilitation team depends on the type of personal relationship established with the stroke patient. Optimism, encouragement and constant reassurance are all essential to this.

All the categories of therapists mentioned are unfortunately in short supply. This has led to the idea that such therapists should be prepared to teach the procedures necessary in any particular case to family and friends.

Speech therapists have been most enthusiastic about this approach. In a recent scheme, volunteer helpers have been used to help patients with severe speech disability. It was noticeable that being visited regularly by enthusiastic volunteers helped the stroke patient to overcome his depression and apathy. Once these were overcome the patient again began to communicate.[15]

THE END RESULT

To help an older person recover slowly from a stroke requires dedication and patience on the part of family and friends. It is encouraging for all concerned to know that many illustrious people have achieved great things after a stroke. Handel wrote the "Messiah" on recovering from a stroke.

Douglas Ritchie has written an interesting account of his own illness in the book *Stroke—A Diary of Recovery*. This book carries an encouraging message of hope for all stroke victims. It also has some practical advice. The use of sliced bread should be encouraged. Men, after a stroke, may find it easier to use an electric razor. Douglas Ritchie mentioned a special code for communication by telephone. A certain number of rings, for example, three, means that a friend or relative is on the line and that he will call again in a couple of minutes. This enables the person recovering from a stroke to get to the telephone after an interval.[16]

AIDS FOR THE DISABLED

Disabilities in one form or another tend to appear as people grow older. The hand becomes less strong, bending is more difficult, finger control is less certain. Quite often medical treatment can improve these conditions. In any case a variety of aids are available nowadays to help people overcome such disabilities.

PROBLEMS WITH DRESSING

Dressing itself can be a problem. Zips may be impossible to handle. In such cases two strips of Velcro, for example one on each side of a skirt, can replace a zip. A simple dressing stick can be made from a coat hanger with the hook removed. A stationer's rubber thimble at one end of the curved stick will cling to the clothes and a notch cut into the other end of the stick helps with pulling up shoulder straps.

Dressing stick made of coathanger

A variety of pick-up sticks are available for people who find bending difficult. The pick-up stick can be used for personal activity such as pulling on stockings and also for household activities such as switching on the light, drawing curtains and operating window catches. Objects can be picked up from the floor or from a table or shelf.[17]

Shoes fitted with elastic laces can be put on more easily, particularly when a long handled shoe horn is used as well.

HAVING AIDS INSTALLED

People who are physically disabled, e.g. after a stroke or as a result of arthritis, are particularly at risk from the point of view of falling and injuring themselves. Under the Chronically Sick and Disabled Persons Act 1970, social services departments are encouraged to provide advice on the aids that can be installed and the improvements that can be under-taken, in an old person's house to promote increased mobility. These aids include hand rails beside stairs and in the toilet, substituting ramps for steps, altering the height of the lavatory, widening doors and raising electric sockets. The old person may have difficulty in getting in and out of the bath. The aids available for this purpose have been described in the section on "The Bathroom".

A wide variety of equipment for medical and nursing purposes—walking frames, bed cradles and back rests—can be supplied on loan from the local authority and in some areas from the local branch of the Red Cross. New bedding can be obtained at a subsidised cost, or even free, if the need is demonstrated. In many instances the family doctor will have to be consulted in order to have his assessment of the situation. These aids and

improvements will play a big part in allowing the old person to retain his
independence.

ELECTRIC AIDS

The Electricity Council has produced an excellent free leaflet *Electric
Aids for Disabled People*. Among other things it mentions alternative
switches that can be used in place of the standard light switch. These
include rocker switches which can be installed at virtually any level and
can be operated by a walking stick, elbow or knee. Pullcord switches are
also available. They can be operated without the need for gripping, for
example by the use of a walking stick.[18]

WALKING TROLLIES

For some elderly people it may be worth considering the temporary
use of a walking trolley. This can act as a combined walking aid and food
trolley.[19]

TELEPHONE

It would be marvellous if every old person in Britain living alone had a
telephone provided, either free or subsidised. This must remain a utopian
idea for the moment. In some cases, however, because of the nature of
an old person's disability, the social services department will sanction the
installation of a telephone, the cost being borne by the local authority.
The old person would then be able to summon help for himself should
a crises arise. The subject of telephones is dealt with in more detail in
Chapter 6.

HELP FOR THE DISABLED

As mentioned earlier the Dsiabled Living Foundation (D.L.F.) any
the Scottish Information Service for the Disabled (S.I.S.D.) will readild
provide information to members of the public regarding aids.[3]

"Those leisure pursuits one has been thinking about for years".

The companionship of pets.

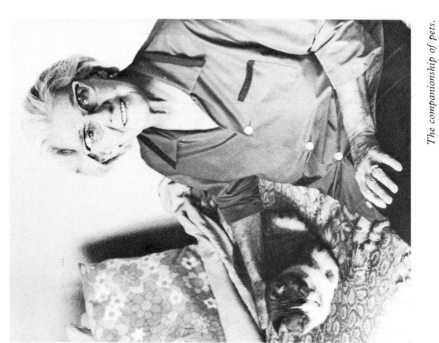

The companionship of pets.

Members of Old People's Clubs—run for pensioners by pensioners.

A Dining Club.

Visitors are always welcome.

A Chat in the Park.

The Lollipop Man—part-time jobs for pensioners.

*The British Red Cross Society—part-time voluntary workers for the
Library Service in hospitals.*

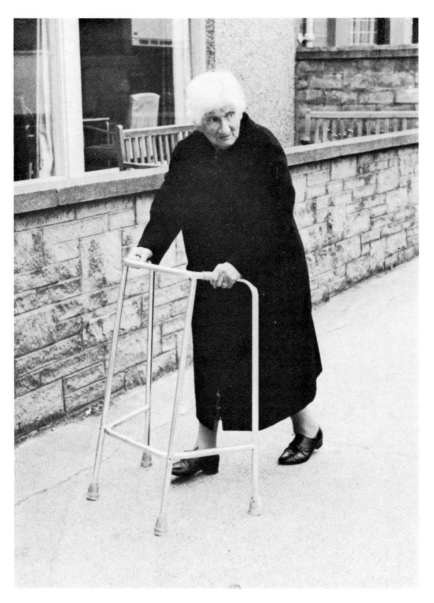

Aids to mobility—a Zimmer frame.

A walking trolley

I would thoroughly recommend the Consumer Publication *Coping with Disablement*. This covers all the difficulties likely to be encountered by the elderly and the disabled. This book reminds us that, when faced with a disability problem, the solution can often lie in seeking an alternative approach rather than in being provided with an aid.[20]

Much progress has been made over the last ten years in the fight to enable disabled people to retain a measure of control over their domestic environment. An inspiring book, *Aids for the Severly Handicapped*, has recently been publihsed describing the several types of highly sophisticated apparatus available for the use of the severly handicapped.[21]

The Disablement Income Group (D.I.G.) believes in a National Disability Income being paid as a right to all disabled people. D.I.G. campaigns continuously for this and also for improvement in all the facilities available to disabled people.[22]

CONTROL OF BLADDER AND BOWEL

HUMILIATION

Difficulties in the control of bladder and bowel tend to be somewhat common among elderly people. Certainly the involuntary escape of urine or emptying of the bowels is a very distressing and humiliating experience. The elderly man or woman suffering from such a difficulty is liable to restrict, to an intolerable degree, usual daily activities. This in turn can have an adverse effect on the morale.

BLADDER WEAKNESS

Let us look first at the more common problem, that of faulty bladder control in an old person.

The relative responsibility for the old person must, of course, approach the matter with a great deal of tact and sensitivity.

In every case it is important to ask the advice of the family doctor. He will be able to arrange the correct medical treatment for those situations that are recoverable. Bladder infections, for example, are usually effectively and simply corrected by taking the appropriate antibiotic.

GETTING TO THE TOILET QUICKLY

Many old people need to get to the toilet without delay once the bladder has become full.

Any old person with this difficulty deserves special sympathy and support. A lack of appreciation of the exact nature of the problem by all concerned can lead to unnecessary accidents. Where mobility is restricted, the usual dash to the toilet would not be possible. Again, certain emotional states, such as resentment and sorrow, can make this symptom worse. If there is a communication difficulty say in the presence of impaired speech after a stroke, this so called "urgency" can be a major problem.

A regular toilet routine should be observed. The old person is encouraged to visit the toilet, even as often as every two hours if necessary. A commode may be required. Walking equipment can help increase mobility. A wise precaution is for evening drinks to be strictly rationed.

TEMPORARY LOSS OF BLADDER CONTROL

It is socially disastrous when all bladder control is lost. Doctors call this incontinence. Here the brain abandons its overall regulating role. As a consequence, the bladder functions completely on its own. There are sudden, frequent, and involuntary emptyings of the bladder.

Complete loss of bladder control may be a temporary condition. After a minor stroke, a period of unconsciousness often occurs. At that time incontinence of urine and loss of bowel control are commonly present. It is usual for some degree of recovery to occur after this phase. The extent to which control of bladder and bowel remain impaired depends on the extent of any brain damage.

PERMANENT LOSS OF BLADDER CONTROL

This tends to occur particularly in senility (see page 116). Fortunately modern technology enables us to cope very adequately with the resulting problems in the home setting. This means that hospitalisation need not always be the inevitable end result.

By inserting a catheter into the bladder, and fixing it in place, the problem can be solved with some degree of satisfaction. It is, in fact, possible for a catheter to be left in place for several months. The bladder in such cases would be drained off every two hours or so. Naturally it is slightly uncomfortable and, also, there is a risk of inducing an infection. This therefore is not an ideal solution.

There are available, both for men and women, dribbling bags made of polythene, which are fixed so as to catch the urine at the outlet from the bladder. The apparatus available for women is still at the experimental stage.

INCONTINENCE PADS

But for most cases of permanent urinary incontinence in men and women some type of incontinence pad is used. These pads are available on prescription from the family doctor. The district nurse will show relatives how to obtain the best results from their use. It should thus be possible to keep a patient warm and dry, providing the pads are changed sufficiently often.[23]

Incontinence pads have to be kept in place by the use of plastic pants, where the old person is up and about. However, they can cause excessive perspiration. This may result in bedsores. For this reason, attention should be paid at all times to local hygiene. The private parts should be washed twice a day with water. As an additional measure the skin should be protected with a silicone barrier cream, such as "Vasogen".

The use of Kanga Pants should be given serious consideration in any ambulant old person with persistent urinary incontinence. These special pants were developed in response to the need for a garment that enables an incontinent person to remain dry. They also overcome the problems of social embarrassment and spoilt clothes.

The garment consists of an "underpant" made of 100% knitted polyester. Kanga Pants fit the body like a swimming costume. Fitted on the outside of the pant is a pouch, plastic-coated on the inside to make it waterproof. Special incontinence pads are inserted into this pouch. Urine passes through the open knit structure of the pants into the pad.

The manufacturers recommend that the pads be changed an average of four times a day. The Kanga Pants should be changed once a day usually. In order to allow for washing and drying, each old person should be provided with three sets of Kanga Pants.

The disposal of incontinence pads at home is often a real problem. The manufacturers of Kanga Pants recommend that the pad is disposed of by tearing open the outer cover and disposing of the flock contents into the W.C. The outer cover has to be disposed of by other means, as a blockage would occur if it was dropped into the W.C.[24]

ALTERING GARMENTS

Old people who suffer from a physical disability in addition to a weak bladder, may find tha tthe usual openings and fastenings in garments are difficult to operate. By a few simple adjustments one can make it easier for an old person to dress and undress. These measures in turn can help the old person to retain his independence.[25]

LOSS OF BOWEL CONTROL

This is a much less common problem than loss of bladder control. It can occur in infections of the bowel. Also, constipation paradoxically may sometimes be responsible. The wall of the lower bowel in this situation loses its normal sensitivity and fails to indicate to the brain when it is "bowel opening" time. The bowel contents become hard and immobile. Frequent and involuntary bowel movements occur. By eating fruit, porridge, vegetables and similar bulk foods regularly this complication can be avoided. The use of a regular laxative, such as "Senokot", might also be indicated.

Elderly people can also prevent sluggishness of the bowels by regularly adding unprocessed pure bran to their morning cereals. Bran consists of the husks that are removed from wheat germ in the process of making white flour. Supplies of bran can be obtained from any health food store. Allison's "Bran Plus" is one variety. As much as two dessertspoonfuls each morning may be necessary. It is best though to start off with a little amount and build up slowly.

LAUNDRY SERVICE

Where a local authority provides a laundry service for incontinent patients the district nurse would be able to give information on this.

CHAPTER 6

Communications

Both keeping in touch and getting help in an emergency are of great concern to the elderly. Fortunately we live in a technological age and modern means of communication are available—in addition to the traditional direct voice—ears—eyes methods.

TELEPHONES

The view has already been expressed elsewhere that ideally no elderly person living at home should be without a telephone. This would apply whether or not the old person was living by himself.

An interesting study was recently conducted in Hull on the value of giving telephones to the elderly housebound. The fact that Hull has its own independent telephone service made it an obvious place for the research.

The results showed that the provision of subsidised or free telephone installation can make a tremendous difference to the lives of people who are old, housebound and poor. It was noted that the elderly people involved in the project felt much less lonely and were also able to summon help more readily in an emergency.[1]

The Post Office is eager to help in any situation where an elderly person is handicapped by one disability or another. The Descriptive Leaflet *Help for the Handicapped* (D.L.E. 550), indicates the telephone aids that are available for various disabled groups. These are the hard of hearing, those with a speech problem, the blind and those with impaired mobility.

When making an enquiry all you have to do is to call the operator and ask for the Telephone Sales Office. The Post Office is anxious to give each request individual attention so that the telephone installation is tailored to the needs of the individual concerned.

So, whether it's an extra telephone by the bedside, an amplifying telephone hand set or a telephone with a special lamp signalling arrangement that seems to be needed, ask the Post Office for their advice.[2]

INTERCOMS

These are systems whereby an elderly person can communicate with a person in another part of the same house, with someone at the front door or even with people living close by in the same street. Depending on what is required, installation costs vary.

Interlock systems for the Disabled is only one of the firms producing this type of equipment. They produce an "Intercom + Door-Lock" kit. This has been devised for those who cannot see who is at the door. It comprises a lightweight battery operated hand-unit with three buttons to allow two-way communication with the caller and the facility of unlocking the door. The hand-unit is easily carried from room to room and plugged into a specially installed connector box in each room where connection is required. The ability to deal with callers at the door in this way can help to give peace of mind to those using this type of equipment.[3]

The equipment produced by Interlock Systems is inexpensive and for the most part simply plugs in, thus requiring no installation. One of these is an intercom which plugs into the power outlets and offers communication from room to room, and even on occasions from house to house.

Disabled Living Foundation Aids Centre has a complete list of firms specialising in Intercom units.[4]

ALARM SYSTEMS

Emergency alarm systems help to give the elderly and handicapped a sense of security and to provide immediate help in an emergency. Traditionally, old people in a fix have relied on banging on a neighbour's wall with a walking stick or blowing a whistle. These methods are still useful but have been supplemented by systems of varying degrees of sophistication.

TYPES OF ALARM SYSTEMS

There are three basic types of alarm systems. (a) Those systems using visual and audible signals. Putting a card in the window with the words "HELP" is an example. Some old people, however, might not be too happy about such a system. They would be afraid that their vulnerability could be exploited. There's also a flashing lights system whereby a touch of a switch or the pulling of a cord operates a flashing light in the window. Some units incorporate a bell either instead of, or as well as, the flashing light. (b) Interruption of routine alarms. This is where the householder must take some positive action to prevent the alarm being set off. One of these is used in connection with the lavatory cistern. If the lavatory has not been flushed for a period of 12 hours, a warning light located in a place where it can be noticed comes on. (c) Body-worn aids. These are portable alarms which run off batteries and which sound an alarm when a button is pressed or a pin pulled. An excellent portable alarm is the Alex Personal Alarm, which only weighs 5 oz. When a pin attached to a cord is pulled out of the unit it gives off a shattering noise—it makes an excellent anti-mugging device! Arthritic hands, of course, might find it not too easy to remove the pin.[5]

Two final points about the alarm systems. First, for any scheme to be successful there has to be regular checking of batteries and equipment. Secondly, any alarm system will fail unless there is cooperation and interest from the local community.

COMMUNITY CARE ALARM SYSTEM

I should like to mention two enterprising organisations that are engaged in research into methods for improving the standard of care available to elderly people living at home.

Davis Safety Controls has devised a "Homecall" system, which is

Alarm systems

claimed to be a viable alternative to institutional care. "Homecall" depends on the local authority providing a trained warden who maintains contact and, in emergency, is summoned by a special unit linked to a telephone, even if the old person cannot move.

The "Homecall" comprehensive telephone link communication system includes re-channelling of calls to the warden wherever she may be (and even by pocket radio if she is out visiting). In certain circumstances the communication system could involve a health visitor, social worker or occupational therapist, rather than a warden.[6]

Cass Electronics has devised a community care alarm system based on the device used to "bleep" doctors in hospital. Basically it consists of a simple radio link between the old person's home and a co-ordinating office at the social services department. The unit for the old person just plugs into a mains socket. If necessary, it can be moved from one room to another. In the event of any difficulties the old person pushes a red alarm button. The operator at the social services department would automatically know the source of the call.[7]

CHAPTER 7

Those Responsible for the Elderly

OFFICIAL COMMUNITY SERVICES

THE FAMILY DOCTOR

The family doctor (general practitioner or G.P.) is a vital person in the maintenance of an old person's health and welfare. The doctor is often involved in activity which is not directly to do with medical care. The doctor provides the medical certificates needed for National Insurance sickness benefits and other insurance claims. His recommendation is necessary for a variety of things,.e.g. most hospital treatment, a home visit from a hospital specialist and the services of a home help or a district nurse.

All G.P.s are listed by the local Family Practitioner Committee (in Scotland by the General Medical Practitioners Committee). This list is available at the local post office but the doctor is not compelled to accept everyone who wishes to register with him.

In common with every other service provided for the elderly in the community, general practice has its critics. It has been pointed out that the appointments system tends to put old people at a disadvantage. But this need not be so, for most practices will endeavour to make allowances in their system to suit the convenience of the elderly patient. There is now a tendency for doctors to work in group practices, which may mean that the elderly person won't necessarily be able to consult their own particular doctor. But should this happen the doctor is usually kept informed of the old person's progress. In most cases, however, it is possible to see the doctor of a patient's choice.

As a result of their medical training, many doctors are conditioned to expect that treating an acute illness in young people is more interesting than attending to the ailments of the elderly. This situation is beginning to change. Looking after the special needs of old people can be very rewarding.

Surveys have shown that most cases of serious illness in the elderly are in fact known to their family doctors. What, however, is often "hidden" is a mass of minor disorders. These can result in serious lack of mobility, comfort and enjoyment.

Detecting these less serious, but none-the-less disabling, ailments should ideally be the task of every general practitioner. Such an approach requires an increase in available resources.

To undertake this "early-warning system", some practices maintain a register of patients who are over 65 years of age. Regular visits, perhaps by a health visitor attached to the practice, would then be possible.

Another, and still more idealistic scheme, involves the establishment of a retirement clinic. It has been suggested that a retirement check-up should take its place, alongside the school medical examination, as a routine part of everyone's way of life. Any abnormalities discovered by the G.P. would be followed-up, possibly by referral to a consultant.[1]

Should an elderly person wish to change his family doctor this is done simply by going to the preferred doctor and asking him if he is willing to accept the application. It might, of course, be to the patient's advantage to discuss any alleged grievance with his former G.P. first. Alternatively the medical card should be sent to the Administrator of the Family Practitioner Committee of the Area Health Authority serving your locality—the address is on the medical card—with a note requesting a change of doctor. In Scotland the procedure is to write to the Administrator of the Primary Care Division of the Health Board for the area. It is always good manners to inform the previous doctor of any action taken.

THE HEALTH VISITOR

The health visitor is a very important member of the health team. The work of the health visitor has changed in its emphasis in recent years.

Originally the bulk of the work was with mothers and young children. Today more time is spent with the physically and mentally handicapped and the old. In rural areas the health visitor is often the midwife and district nurse as well.

A very valuable supportive and preventive service can be provided by a health visitor. She can advise on diet, budgeting, prevention of accidents and the various community facilities available for the elderly. On her own initiative she may arrange for a home help or a voluntary visitor to call.

An increasing number of health visitors are attached to health centres and to group practices of general practitioners.[2]

THE DISTRICT NURSE

The therapeutic side of domiciliary nursing is undertaken by the district nurse. Under the direction of the family doctor the district nurse undertakes treatments such as changing dressings, giving injections, administering enemas and helping to wash and bath a patient. She may teach a patient or his family how to carry out some forms of treatment. If incontinence is a problem, the nurse might arrange for disposable incontinence pads to be made available. In addition, where the local authority is responsible for an incontinent laundry service, relatives would be put in touch with this. The frequency of the district nurse's visits will vary according to the needs of each case.[3]

THE PSYCHIATRIC NURSE

In recent years there has been an increasing shift in emphasis, in the management of psychiatric illness, from hospital care to that based on the community. In practice this means that elderly people are discharged home, after in-patient psychiatric treatment, at an earlier stage than used to be the case. Support and care of a professional kind is very necessary in such circumstances—for patient and relative alike. Fortunately in many areas nurses from the psychiatric hospital regularly visit elderly patients after discharge.

This domiciliary psychiatric nurse service is very valuable from several points of view. Of particular importance is the fact that the psychiatric nurse already knows, and is accepted by, the patient. This relationship is crucial and can be used to encourage an elderly person. Note is made by the psychiatric nurse of any difficulties resulting from the taking of pills, such as drug side effects. Helpful advice and support can be given to relatives. The psychiatric nurse reports regularly to the family doctor and the psychiatrist on the progress of any particular patient.

HOSPITAL SERVICES

The hospital services, both in-patient and out-patient, are much used by elderly people. About half of the patients admitted to the general wards of hospitals are over 60. In some areas there exists a geriatric unit, which is either a special hospital or a separate department in a general hospital, designed for the needs of older people. The service provided is partly preventive and partly therapeutic. Day hospitals for elderly patients are a fairly recent development. They are usually sited in hospitals. Patients who have been recently discharged attend on one or more days each week.

Elderly people with nervous disorders may be referred by the family doctor for the opinion of a psychiatrist. The consultation can take place at an out-patient clinic or in the old person's home.

Any old person admitted to hospital is sure to appreciate visits from relatives and friends. Do not lose interest in any elderly person you visit regularly just because he is a hospital patient for a while.

I would like to stress one particular point for any relative responsible for an elderly person about to be discharged from hospital. This concerns "What the doctor wants me to do". Often an old person, because of a state of excitement is unable to fully understand—never mind remember —what the hospital specialist says about the taking of pills, the desired degree of activity and such like. No doctor, if tactfully asked, will mind providing written instructions about aftercare.

THE REMEDIAL PROFESSIONS

The work of physiotherapists, occupational therapists, speech therapists and dieticians is still largely centred on general hospitals. In recent years, however, the remedial professions have been working more and more in day hospitals (see above) and even in patients' homes.[4]

Occupational therapists can play a very crucial part in helping to maintain the independence of old people living at home. At the request of the family doctor an occupational therapist will pay a home assessment visit. An "Activities of Daily Living" (A.D.L.) is undertaken. Unfortunately the service is provided only from Mondays to Fridays. In exceptional circumstances the service is available on Sundays. Advice would then be given on the aids and domestic adjustments considered necessary to enable an elderly person to cope with mobility problems and difficulties in washing, dressing and cooking.

SOCIAL WORKER

The social services department (the social work department in Scotland) provides a wide range of services for the community. The responsibilities of a social worker, attached to a social services department, can range from the supervision of the different types of residential accommodation—for children, the elderly and the homeless—to meeting the needs of society's various under-privileged groups. The local authority accommodation, in which the social services department has an interest, is described in Chapter 8.[5]

HOME HELPS

The home help service is one of the best known of the local authority services. The numbers have been increasing over the past four years. In September 1973 there were in England and Wales 40,738 full time home helps. Unfortunately, the service is provided only from Mondays to Fridays. More public money, and a change of policy, would be required for this to be extended.

Whenever a request for a home help is received at the social services department from a family doctor or a health visitor, the home help organiser visits the house. In this way the most suitable home help can be chosen for the old person concerned.

Home helps are selected for their ability to give the old person a sense

The home help

of security and also for their age ability to tolerate the eccentric behaviour sometimes seen in old age.

The duties of a home help vary accordingly to circumstances. They may include help with dressing, personal toilet and cooking, house cleaning and laundry, shopping and the payment of bills.

Sometimes male home helps are employed and are invaluable for dealing with elderly men.

OTHER OFFICIAL SERVICES

Some areas use auxiliaries. Individuals are chosen to do particular tasks, such as lighting a fire or filling a hot water bottle, for which they are paid.

In some places a paid night sitting-in service, and even an equivalent day service, is available. No nursing is involved, but the sitters help to provide relatives with a periodic welcome break.

Day centres for infirm elderly people are provided by many local authorities. They are not part of the hospital service. Meals and diversional therapy are provided. Transport for the elderly people is needed for this service.

The help that your local Director of Environmental Health, previously called the Sanitary Inspector, can give has been referred to earlier. The Director is responsible for the promotion of healthy living conditions. Emphasis is laid on the provision of an efficient system of refuse collection and disposal. Directors of Environmental Health are also involved in educating and guiding the public with regard to food hygiene, safety in the house, tolerable noise levels and other matters in the realms of preventive medicine.

POSTMEN

In Burnley there has recently been a successful pilot scheme, in which postmen were involved in helping the old. Every housebound person was given a yellow card with the message, "Postman, please call". When one of the elderly people required assistance, the card was displayed in the window. The postman would then look in on his next round to see what sort of help was needed.

VOLUNTARY COMMUNITY SERVICES

It will never be possible—probably not even desirable—for the official services just listed to cover all the needs of the elderly. The gap continues to be filled by the voluntary organisations. In many cases these organisations have pioneered a service that was later taken over officially.

Voluntary organisations have been a part of the British way of life for a long time. In the 1970s, alongside the welfare state, these organisations continue to care for society's less fortunate members. There is an almost limitless fund of goodwill, and potential for constructive action, among the voluntary reserves in Britain.

The voluntary organisations are self-governing. They alone decide what policies to pursue, even though some of their funds come from central government or local authorities.

Voluntary work can take the form of an individual, and personal, service. Alternately, the contributions can be by working alongside others in a co-ordinate community effort.[6]

AGE CONCERN

Age Concern deserves special mention as the national organisation that effectively co-ordinates the work of statutory bodies and voluntary organisations in many parts of the United Kingdom. Age Concern works solely for the welfare of the elderly. It acts as an information centre about services available for old people and it provides training facilities for workers. There are Old People's Welfare Committees that have been set up all over the country by local initiative. These committees are affiliated to the Age Concern headquarters in London, Edinburgh, Cardiff and Belfast.[7]

Age Concern constantly strives to correct the widely held image of old people as passive, poor and pitiful second class citizens. As a dynamic contribution to this, Age Concern has recently published *Manifesto: on the place of the retired and the elderly in modern society*. This document sets out the factors that it believes could, if implemented, improve life for old people in Britain. It deserves to be widely read. Special emphasis is put on the need to consult old people themselves about their social and environmental needs.

RED CROSS AND THE W.R.V.S.

On a nation-wide basis both the Red Cross[8] and the Women's Royal Voluntary Service[9] provide for the elderly. In any area one or other of these two particular organisations is responsible for the meals-on-wheels service. This provides a hot meal, most usually once or twice a week.

The cost of the meals is borne partly by the local authority, partly by the voluntary organisation and partly by the old people themselves (see page 27).

CITIZENS' ADVICE BUREAU

The Citizens' Advice Bureau service is one of the largest voluntary undertakings in the country. Accurate information and skilled advice is provided on a wide range of family and personal problems. The address of your local C.A.B. office can be found by looking in the yellow pages of the Telephone directory or by writing to National Citizens' Advice Bureaux Council.[10]

In each of the four parts of the United Kingdom there is a National Council of Social Service that exists to co-ordinate the work of the statutory welfare authorities and all voluntary organisations by means of consultation and joint action.[11]

THE CHURCHES

The spiritual needs of the elderly are the particular responsibility of the churches. Ministers of religion recognise that a mature faith often carries a measure of agnosticism. The old sometime need reminding and re-assuring.

A man approaching death often wishes to talk to a priest who can listen sympathetically. More comfort often results from this than from the administration of a tranquilliser.

The churches have always looked after the elderly in their midst. This caring attitude persists in the provision of Eventide Homes.

In the midst of our basically materialistic world, we should not forget the importance of faith.

Many old people find it difficult to continue attending church under their own steam. In such circumstances car lifts from other members of the congregation would be much appreciated. The church concerned might even make out a rota of voluntary car drivers.

CHAPTER 8

Problems of the Elderly

PSYCHOLOGICAL CHANGES

Old age is the final adaptation. There is often a variety of things to be accommodated to. There is the possibility of ill-health, such as a minor stroke, a fracture. Changes also occur in the world around us. One of the most significant is the abrupt retirement that faces everyone, especially men. Friends and relatives die. Children have grown up and moved away. Money—always a problem—is tight.

The psychological changes that commonly occur in an old person are, unfortunately, not of a sort generally to make adaptation to these types of difficulties any easier.

LACK OF FLEXIBILITY

Rigidity, together with a tendency to resist change, is very characteristic. There is a reduced ability to deal with complex situations. Black-and-white thinking also occurs. In other words something is seen as being terribly good or terribly bad. There are no grey areas of compromise. These feelings will be particularly strong if the old person is emotionally insecure.

BLAMING OTHERS

Another pattern that is often seen in the old is the tendency to blame others for one's own mistaken attitude or misdoings. This occurs when a

Blaming others

particular act or thought is unacceptable to the individual's conscience. Here's where the wife or husband, the weather or even the government of the day gets all the blame. It's an easy way out. On rare occasions these ideas can lead to serious mental illness (see page 120).

MANIPULATIVE AND MOODY

When life becomes particularly frustrating for an old person, he may "go back in time" and act in an infantile manner. This might occur particularly when the old person feels no longer needed by his children or his friends. Acting up is used as a device to catch the attention of anyone who happens to be about at the time.

Both depression and anxiety are commonly seen in old people, particularly where the stresses of ill-health or environmental changes prove too much. These have been discussed on page 1.

DIFFICULTIES IN UNDERSTANDING

Communication problems are found in old age. These include a lessened understanding, an inability to listen and a weakness of the voice. The capacity for learning is often diminished. These changes are to some degree compensated for by an old person's greater experience of life compared with that of younger people.

To help an old person master these psychological changes, one should encourage friendships and foster interests. Strengths of personality that are present should be built upon.

Friends should be cultivated from a broad base

RETIREMENT

Whether regrettable or not in social terms retirement at 60 and 65, for women and men respectively, is a fact of life. Retirement is marked by a transition from active involvement with people to partial or complete withdrawal from them. This shows the folly of relying entirely on the work situation for fulfilment in a social sense. Friends should be cultivated if possible from a broad base. Also, husbands and wives are well advised to have friends of their own, as well as in common. Otherwise the early death of one's spouse can lead to the remaining one being very isolated.

THE CONSEQUENCES OF RETIREMENT

Apart from the loss of friends, retirement brings a change in status. We are living in times, in which the value of old people has come into question. The skills, knowledge and attitudes that were relevant in an old person's youth and middle age are often sadly rendered obsolete by the technical and social advances of today. Young people may no longer respect their elders. The wisdom of elderly people gathered over a life-time sometimes carries little weight with the younger generation. Old people sense this lack of respect and consequently may feel alienated and generally useless.

The relatively low status old people appear to have in our society is also the result of their low spending power and the loss of their functions as breadwinners and parents.

On the other hand, retirement brings a time of relative freedom from responsibilities. It also heralds a time to pursue those leisure pursuits one may have been thinking about for years. This tends to be a pious hope if there's been no preparation for retirement.

PRE-RETIREMENT COURSES

Some years ago it was realised that the hazards and frustrations of retired life can be managed with a little forethought. This is the basis of "Preparation for Retirement" courses. Employees nearing retirement are encouraged to attend these on a day release basis. Subjects covered are the basic ones, such as medical care, diet, living on lower incomes, hobbies, recreation, clothes and transport. Planning how to occupy those forty to fifty hours a week previously spent at work is given particular emphasis.

The Pre-Retirement Association (P.R.A.) has been active in this field for many years. They run several types of pre-retirement advisory courses.

Leisure pursuits one has been thinking about for years

Many of these are held in cooperation with industrial and commercial firms and also state enterprises. A course for pre-retirement tutors has recently been established.

In addition the P.R.A. works hard at educating the public about the valuable contribution that retired people can continue to make to society. A monthly magazine is published, *Pre-Retirement Choice*.[1]

LEADING A FULL LIFE

What exactly constitutes "a good life" for a retired person? Basically, it is a life that is challenging, meaningful and satisfying. A more specific definition is provided in a recently published book.[2] The normal healthy man or woman in retirement is said to need ACTIVITY in physical and mental terms, CREATIVITY to ward off staleness, CONTACT with other generations and groups and a real living sense of PURPOSE.

There are several organisations that are actively trying to promote, in one way or another, the interests of pensioners as a group in the community.

The British Pensioners and Trade Union Action Committee is engaged in fighting for a decent living pension for all pensioners. This organisation is active North of the border as the Scottish Old Age Pensions Association.[3]

The British Association of Retired Persons, B.A.R.P., acts as a voice for those retired people existing on a fixed or almost fixed income.[4]

For many years the National Federation of Old Age Pensions Association has striven to improve conditions for old people in the United Kingdom. It produces a lively weekly paper, *Pensioners' Voice.*[5]

Help the Aged produces a newspaper, *Yours*, eleven times a year. It has a topical agony column for pensioners, "A Trouble Shared". The newspaper is distributed for a nominal sum to pensioners.[6]

There is no doubt that all of these organisations will continue to compaign for a better way of life for pensioners, just as they have done in the past.

SELF-HELP

In recent years there has been evidence of a grass roots movement among the elderly. This is where people become involved in Self-help schemes, in one form or another. Old people have at last realised that there are practical alternatives to just sitting and thinking about problems.

Faced with feelings of isolation and helplessness, pensioners decide to act constructively and organise themselves into Action Groups. The aims of such groups vary. They can range from the replacing of broken pavement stones and the planning of a bulk-buying grocery scheme to the publicising of Welfare Rights Information.

The idea for an Action Group often comes first from a community worker, who knows the local scene. Such a person would provide the initial stimulation required in order to get any particular scheme launched.[7]

BEREAVEMENT

Society is in so many respects better educated, more tolerant and more humane than it ever was. The sad truth, however, is that little attempt is made in so many cases to make more bearable the suffering that results from bereavement. Oddly too, the matter is one that remains, for all our sophistication, taboo.

It is important for all of us to realise that mourning is both necessary and natural. Grief is painful and distressing. It is the price we pay for having loved so deeply the person who is gone. Doctors are usually not anxious to prescribe anti-depressant drugs for a person with a grief reaction unless the depression is of pathological intensity.

THE DEPTH OF GRIEF

The intensity of grief in a particular instance depends on three factors. (a) The suddenness or otherwise of the loss. Where a death has been long foreseen, the reaction will often be one of relief. Faced with a death that is sudden and unexpected the survivor may be overwhelmed. (b) The support and understanding given by others. Friends can provide a real measure of support by sharing the sadness and distress of the bereaved person. This may have to be given for some months or even for years. Naturally support of this type can be draining. Ministers of religion and doctors have to learn how to give support without becoming overwhelmed by the prevailing mood of sadness. Lay people will find this very hard too. (c) The degree of which grief is allowed expression. Anguish and grief must be allowed full expression. Otherwise the bereaved person will find it difficult to accept the finality of the death.

THE STAGES OF GRIEF

In normal circumstances grief lasts for only a few months and is composed of recognisable stages. In the first stage, the predominant attitude is one of disbelief. This stage is usually brief and is followed by a period of depression. Next, in many cases, there follows a stage of apportioning blame. The bereaved person particularly tends to blame himself for not having cared enough. Responsibility is also laid on doctors, nurses or God. It is probably helpful to tactfully remind mourners of the actual facts—of the disabling stroke and the serious pneumonia. The next period is one of slow recovery.

Grief becomes pathological and in need of medical treatment if it lasts more than six months. More women than men experience this illness. Anti-depressants or even psychiatric treatment may be required.

Sympathetic and supportive friends can help mourners to cope with the consequences of bereavement other than grief. These are the social and emotional problems, the stigma of pity and the avoidance by people who "don't want to know".

PRACTICAL MEASURES

In view of the fact that widows outnumber widowers, married couples should bear two particular points in mind. First, both spouses should be aware of the financial and legal situation that would result when one of the pair dies. Secondly, a retirement house should be chosen for its suitability for a frail widow.

Cruse Clubs is an organisation with many local branches throughout Britain that exists to help widows combat feelings of loneliness and desperation.[8] Practical advice is also offered by this society.

The National Association of Widows has a counselling and advisory service. It also strives to remove anomalies in the circumstances facing widows.[9]

Mrs. Sarah Morris was widowed a few years ago. Discovering that no book had been written about grief as it affects the mourner, she proceeded to write her own. The result is a clearly written and helpful book *Grief: and how to live with it*.[10]

THINKING ABOUT ALTERNATIVE ACCOMMODATION

LIVING ALONE AT HOME

Obviously, in most cases an elderly person wishes to continue living in his own house. Experts also now advise old people to think very carefully before moving, say at retirement, to an entirely new district where there are no familiar faces. One's friends are always a very precious commodity, but particularly so in later years.

Of course, a change in health or some alteration in life's circumstances may force an old person to consider the advisability of carrying on at home on his own.

A word of warning. We must beware of imposing our ideas of "What's right and proper" on elderly people. An old couple in their 80s may find their country cottage, with no proper sanitation or running hot water, a home beyond compare. The fact that we consider their living conditions appalling is no reason for forcibly persuading the old people to tear up their roots to live in a high-rise flat in the nearby town. A sense of perspective has to be kept.

Let us look at the situation where an old person, because of frailty, feels he can no longer cope at home without some form of support. The help that can be provided officially by the community should be borne in mind. The attendance of a home help and the provision of meals-on-wheels can make all the difference to that type of old person. Other services, such as that of the district nurse or a social worker, might also be appropriate. The various community services are described in Chapter 7.

SHARING

Alternatively the old person may wish to share house with a relative, a friend, or even a lodger. Thereby some companionship is provided and also help in times of need.

In such circumstances it might be appropriate for the sons and daughters of the old person to hold a family conference to decide whose house is to be shared. This is a delicate matter requiring a lot of tact. Sons-in-law and daughters-in-law should be involved as well.

Some families, of course, are not accustomed to the type of frank speaking that would be necessary. In that case a doctor, lawyer, social worker or respected friend could be asked to chair any meetings. The income, the state of health, the temperament and the willingness to help of everyone concerned would all have to be considered before a final decision was made.

A son or daughter living in Council accommodation may wish an elderly parent to move in with his family. Permission would have to be obtained from the local authority housing manager. This is because there are regulations governing the number of people who may occupy a Council house.[11]

For a description of the difficulties resulting from three generations living close together under one roof see page 20.

Perhaps the old person would consider some form of letting. Students, young teachers and apprentices on courses are often on the look out for accommodation. One room in the house could be made into a bed-sitter with a small table cooker. The bathroom would be used by arrangement and the kitchen now and again for preparing an elaborate meal.

Where the elderly person's problem is that of having too big a house, consideration should be given to the idea of having it converted into flatlets.

An old person with adequate savings, may wish to consider moving into a small *en-pension* hotel.

LOCAL AUTHORITY ACCOMMODATION

Inevitably there are circumstances where a bit of independence has to be sacrificed and the old person must move into alternative housing. The special accommodation for old people set up by the local authority would probably be considered first.

There are basically two types of housing provided by local authorities for old people. First, there is special housing for the aged in small 1, 1½ or 2 apartment houses. These are situated within general housing schemes and so in this way the elderly are kept within the general community. Secondly, sheltered housing is provided. This involves a number of grouped flatlets, bungalows or converted bedsitters, which are self-contained in themselves. Each sheltered housing scheme has a warden, who is available to help in a general way and also if there is an emergency. Each tenant has a buzzer connected with the warden's accommodation. A common sitting room is often provided. This is a good place for a chat with friends and acquaintances. These schemes enable an old person to retain a good measure of independence.

The local housing manager is responsible for these houses. He will have to be approached in order that an old person's name be put on the waiting list. Unfortunately some elderly people, like a lot of us, are either ignorant of the rules laid down by bureaucracy or just apathetic. This means that someone, perhaps you, must get this done on their behalf.

HOUSING ASSOCIATIONS

Some housing for the elderly is provided by voluntary housing associations. These are non-profit-making bodies concerned with providing rented accommodation.

One of the most well known of these housing associations is The Abbeyfield Society Ltd. This organisation converts moderately sized houses into unfurnished bed-sitting rooms. Each has a housekeeper who is responsible for buying and preparing the two main meals of the day. The meals are served in a communal dining room.[12]

Anchor Housing Association has created many group houses for the elderly.[13]

Housing associations get substantial financial support from the government. They are all affiliated to the National Federation of Housing Societies. The Federation would inform you of the housing associations in your area and of any at the planning stage.[14]

BOARDING-OUT SCHEMES

In some places there are boarding-out schemes in existence. Elderly people, usually on a temporary basis, stay with families in private households. Relatives of an old person may in this way be able to arrange to go on a short holiday with a free conscience.

RESIDENTIAL CARE

Every local authority is obliged by law to provide residential accommodation (Eventide Homes) for those who, because of advanced age or infirmity, are unable to live at home. Some voluntary agencies, such as religious organisations, also provide these.

In a few areas some local authorities have provided Homes for Elderly Mentally Confused. These satisfy a special need.

For general advice on accommodation ask your local Citizens' Advice Bureau, the local authority housing manager or your Old People's Welfare Committee or the social services departments. The social services departments visit their own Eventide Homes and inspect those in their area that are privately run.

CHAPTER 9

Serious Mental Disturbances

It is vitally important that the presence of a serious mental disturbance
in an elderly person is recognised at an early stage. So much unnecessary
misery can result if such conditions are not brought to the attention of the
family doctor. Many of the illnesses concerned are completely curable and
the rest are always controllable by drugs and other means.

Every doctor, nurse and social worker in the community knows that
for every crisis referred, there are perhaps ten or twenty other cases
grumbling away without any type of support, professional or non-
professional.

This is the "tip of the iceberg" phenomenon. The significance of early
evidence of illness is easily missed. This could take the form of a general
slowing up, an unusual preoccupation with death or hearing accusatory
voices.

Let us now examine the disorders that are responsible for most cases
of serious mental disturbance in old age.

DEPRESSION

Half of those who are suffering from a serious mental disturbance in
old age have an illness called Depression. We are not talking here of the
periodic emotional upset—the occasional off day, the fleeting blue spell—
which all of us experience. That's part and parcel of everyday life!

The depressed mood in a person with a depressive illness is one of
pathological degree, similar in fact to what has been called melancholia.
Another typical feature is the prolonged nature of the mood disorder.

Typically the depression in this type of illness persists for weeks or months after an episode that would, in most people, have resulted in only a temporary upset.

CAUSES OF DEPRESSION

On many occasions the reasons for depression are easily identified. Commonly a bereavement is responsible. Grown-up children, pre-occupied with their own family problems, may fail to keep in regular contact. Or a close friend of many years standing may move for a variety of reasons, such as change of job or retirement to another area. Older people are less able to cope with such stresses than those of younger years. Physical illness, e.g. a stroke or bronchitis, often results in a state of depression. This, too, can occur after certain types of drugs have been used.

Quite often, however, serious Depressions occur out of the blue, there being no obvious reason for the state of distress.

THE EFFECTS OF DEPRESSION

A person suffering from Depression is no longer able to enjoy life, not even to the slightest degree. They cannot be jollied out of their misery. Thoughts come slowly. Conversation gets slowed up and may become monosyllabic or non-existent. A person with Depression becomes pre-occupied with morbid matters. The ill person appears to be "wrapped up in a black cloud". Bodily movements become affected. Arms and legs move slowly and may seem robot-like. The face, in advanced cases, becomes mask-like and unresponsive. Bodily functions tend to slow up. This results in poor appetite, loss of weight and constipation. Accompanying these changes there may be a hypochondriacal outlook.

Suicidal thoughts may be expressed. This can often be in a disguised form. An elderly depressed person, for example, may indicate his frame of mind by cancelling a long planned holiday, by refusing to see old friends or by changing a will. What is remarkable to the outsider is the degree to which the depressed person changes in his behaviour and outlook. Equally important is the fact that the old person affected may not realise he is ill. He therefore does not even consider asking for help from his doctor.

Serious cases of Depression develop other features. Commonly there is a feeling of guilt, sometimes to a pathological degree, regarding some past misdeameanour of a trivial nature. The person feels worthless and often insists he should be punished. Such statements should be regarded with great seriousness. This may indicate that the person sees suicide as the "only way out".

In the past any elderly person who was obviously unwell in a mental or psychiatric sense was regarded as being senile. We now know that this does not represent the real situation. As I said earlier, half the old people with a serious mental disturbance are suffering from Depression.

Depression will usually lift spontaneously, but sometimes this can take many months, even years. It is therefore important to see that depressed patients receive treatment and that they receive it early.

TREATMENT

Doctors may advise elderly patients with Depression to go into a psychiatric hospital for a few weeks. There are several reasons for this. Close observation and supervision are often necessary initially. These can only be provided in a hospital setting. Also, depressed patients often eat an inadequate diet. They need building up. Lastly, it is important that any other medical conditions, apart from the Depression, are properly managed. A diabetic state might be out of control, a rheumatic condition might be temporarily worse, an eyesight problem (e.g. cataract) might require to be reviewed.

Treatment of the Depression itself takes three forms:

First, drugs are often prescribed. The most important of these are the antidepressants. They are very effective and work by reversing the mood disorder. Sedatives are also given where agitation and restlessness are features of the illness. Sleeping tablets might be prescribed initially for insomnia, a common complaint in Depression.

Secondly, E.C.T. (commonly known as electric shock treatment) can be used on a twice weekly basis in some cases. It is very commonly employed and also is extremely safe even when administered to old people.

Thirdly, the patient has discussions with the psychiatrist and the nurses responsible for his care. This is psychotherapy. The depressed person is encouraged to talk about his feelings and his problems in a relaxed and confidential setting. It is hoped that in this way he will eventually be able to see his difficulties in a newer, more realistic and more hopeful light.

So, if you know an elderly person who appears to you to be suffering from Depression, report the matter to the family doctor concerned. Do not delay.

Remember—Depression is curable.

Depression is curable

SENILITY

This is what doctors refer to as dementia. The fundamental feature of Senility is a pronounced, persistent and progressive loss of memory for recent events.

This forgetfulness comes about because the brains cells are weakened by a disease process of one sort or another. This often takes the form of hardening of the arteries. This particular condition causes not only Senility but also strokes and heart failure.

Characteristically in a person with Senility, what happened last month, last week, yesterday or even that very morning is either not recalled at all or else recalled in a vague and incorrect way. By contrast there is usually an ability to recall, even vividly, the events of long ago, such as childhood.

In an extreme form the memory loss can result in the failure, on the part of the old person, to recognise friends of long standing and even close relatives. This development in turn can lead to embarrassment and tensions within the household. A devoted daughter-in-law might be referred to as "that woman in the kitchen". Clearly a great deal of tact and understanding is needed in the handling of such situations.

COMPENSATING FOR MEMORY LOSS

Initially elderly people with Senility are able to compensate for their forgetfulness (see page 23). They preserve an air of normality and of knowing it all. They reply to questions briefly as they realise a fuller answer might reveal their difficulties.

Later the compensation may break down. The memory problem is often associated with a difficulty in concentration. This in turn results in things going astray—spectacles, the household purse. False accusations may then be made against a relative or even a friendly visitor.

NEGLECT

The senile person is apt to neglect himself to some degree. This usually means that he looks less trim and is also less houseproud. Along with this there may be a tendency to withdraw from people, to become isolated. At an even later stage in Senility the old person concerned is liable to have phases of restlessness. This may show itself by constant hand wringing or even by an inability to sit down during a visit. The elderly person may turn "night into day" and perhaps start to clean the house in the middle of the night. Neighbours may be repeatedly disturbed as a result of nocturnal visits from the old person.

Weakness of bladder or bowel, or both, may develop (see page 82). If a commode is provided, this will help to reduce the number of accidents. It is sensible to remember to take old people regularly to the lavatory, particularly after meals.

SUPPORT FOR THE FAMILY

It should be stressed that the type of Senility seen in most old people is only mild in form. This means that the elderly person concerned can usually remain at home. By your concern, enthusiasm and practical approach you can play a vital part in (a) allowing the old person with failing memory to remain at home and (b) helping him to keep in touch. This second aspect has a direct bearing on the elderly person's quality of life and needs, in my view, to be emphasised time and time again.

Quite often an old person with Senility is cared for at home by his own family. Relatives are usually prepared to continue caring for the elderly person providing:

(a) Their difficulties are appreciated by the family doctor, district nurse and friends and that they can be allowed to talk of the problems to someone sympathetic;

(b) The burden is shared.

It is the prospect of nursing an ailing relative indefinitely without relief that results in families experiencing despair.

Visits from health visitors, or in some cases, psychiatric nurses from the local psychiatric hospital, can afford great support to relatives. Often an old person with Senility can visit a day hospital or a day centre several times a week. This helps to prevent such an old person becoming withdrawn and apathetic.

In some cases there is available a "granny-sitting" service at the local residential home. By arrangement with the matron, relatives can leave an old person watching television with other old people, while they go out for the evening.

Relatives should also be aware of the possibility of arranging for an old person with Senility to be temporarily admitted to a ward in a geriatric or psychiatric hospital so that they can go on holiday. The family doctor would give you details.

Particular care is of course necessary where the old person lives on his own. A greater frequency of visits would be essential in order to watch over the situation. There would be no need for lengthy conversations on each occasion—just a friendly greeting and a smile.

CONVERSATION

Frankly, conversation with an elderly person with Senility is at times no easy matter. During a chat he may suddenly stare ahead, obviously lost in "another world". There can be a tendency to be repetitious. This can be irritating and even embarrassing. Try not to be put off. Old people, like others, can sense when you are losing interest (see page 11).

WHEN TO GET MEDICAL ADVICE

Where an old person's forgetfulness is rapidly worsening, the family doctor should be informed. For obvious reasons severe memory loss can constitute a danger to life and limb. I am thinking particularly of risks from fire or gas (see pages 27 and 51).

In essence then, when you are uncertain whether or not an old person with memory loss can cope at home any longer, discuss the matter with the health visitor, social worker or family doctor.

Once an assessment has been made by the doctor the person may be admitted for observation to a geriatric hospital or a psychiatric hospital. Appropriate medical care can be given and also the support that is necessary from nursing and other staff.

Quite often, where the forgetfulness is only of a moderate degree, the elderly person can be accommodated in local authority residential accommodation.

DELIRIUM

THE REASONS FOR DELIRIUM

This is a serious medical condition that can affect a person of any age. There are numerous causes. Infections are particularly liable to lead to Delirium. Indeed, delirious states in a large percentage of the elderly result from infections of the lungs, such as bronchitis or pneumonia. Another common cause in old people is heart failure for one reason or another. Less common causes include anaemia, vitamin deficiency and a diabetic state that is out of control. Don't forget, too, that whenever an alcoholic's supply of drink runs out there is a real danger of withdrawal symptoms developing—in the form of delirium tremens.

Hypothermia (see page 30) and the development of a brain clot following a head injury, perhaps some days or weeks previously, are other conditions that can be responsible.

Disease, then, in various forms can cause Delirium. Drugs taken by an elderly person can at times also lead to this condition. Older people, for instance, tend to be unusually sensitive to some types of medicine. Barbiturates, taken in the form of sleeping tablets, are particularly liable to cause a temporary mixed up state after rising the next morning. Doctors generally try to prescribe the lowest possible dose of any drug for an elderly person in order to reduce such adverse reactions.

An additional hazard arises when the advice given by the doctor about a particular medicine is misunderstood. To take a specific example, the verbal instructions, "Take this three times a day" is very similar to "Take three of these once a day". Should the old person be on several different types of pills, the risk of a Delirium developing as a result of a misunderstanding will be greatly increased (see page 64).

THE EFFECTS OF DELIRIUM

Let me now describe to you in more detail the state of Delirium. Basically it is a fluctuating state of half-consciousness in which vivid hallucinations may be experienced. An hallucination is something that is seen or heard, but that has no objective reality. Hallucinations in Delirium are most often visual. People, for example, not actually present may be "seen" in the room. Conversation may be held with such imagined persons.

There tends to be a marked variation in the level of Delirium at different times of the day. Often there is a characteristic worsening of the condition towards evening. In Delirium, considerable fear and anxiety is often experienced.

In most cases of Delirium the illness has an abrupt start. There will have been little or no mental impairment prior to the onset of the Delirium. This is a very important point and helps to differentiate Delirium from the slow insidious process of Senility.

TREATMENT

If you suspect that an elderly person has Delirium, do not delay in arranging for the doctor to call. Delirious patients need urgent attention. Often treatment can only be given adequately in hospital. Appropriate medical care given early will ensure a rapid and often a complete recovery.

PARANOID REACTIONS

BLAMING OTHERS

The tendency to blame others and not oneself is a common human failing. As people grow older this tendency becomes more pronounced. This has already been referred to on page 100.

Psychologists are able to explain the particular liability of old people to this development. They say it is the loneliness, the general insecurity and the infirmities, especially deafness, of old age that bear this responsibility.

Elderly people as a result of such deprivations tend to feel as if they were living in a vast empty space. This feeling is compensated for by the creation of a fantasy world. Persecutory beliefs, also called paranoid ideas, become evident.

Thus an old woman may feel that neighbours are talking about her, that policemen are watching her or that relatives are trying to poison her. Sometimes these persecutory beliefs are accompanied by the experience of hearing voices, otherwise known as auditory hallucinations.

It tends to be people that are geographically or emotionally close to the old person that get the blame.

Usually such situations can be coped with as a result of sympathy and understanding. When you offer friendship to an old person with paranoid ideas you are helping to restore his self-esteem. This, in turn, may reduce the need for the fantastic beliefs. Practical measures should also be considered. Renewing spectacles or a hearing aid may be relevant. Ensuring that the lighting in the older person's house is adequate can be important.

SERIOUS ACCUSATIONS

On rare occasions an old person's paranoid ideas may be so persistent or so bizarre that hospitalisation will be required. This might be necessary, for example, where an elderly person felt he was under the hypnotic influence of another person.

Such an occurrence would indicate the onset of a serious mental illness. Studies have shown that unmarried women are particularly susceptible to this. The level of awareness of the affected person is quite unaltered by this disease. Also, it is characteristic that the condition occurs without a history of preceeding stress of any sort.

A paranoid illness in an old person tends to be of long duration Fortunately it does not carry any threat to life. Nowadays doctors are able to quickly remove paranoid symptoms by using tranquillisers. Such drugs have to be given for long periods of time for the improvement to be lasting.

MANIA

Mania is a state of unnatural and unwarranted joyfulness. This not very common illness, which affects all age groups, is closely related to the state of serious depression described earlier in this chapter. Mania is indeed a direct mirror image of depression.

The person affected feels exalted and optimistic. Moreover, he fails to understand why others do not share his feelings of optimism. At times, his benevolent attitude gives way to an outburst of irritability and rudeness.

A manic person is extremely active, writing letters, making plans, telephoning friends and talking endlessly. He usually needs little sleep, but does not appear to suffer as a consequence.

The general picture of restlessness and boisterousness is often complicated by heavy drinking and gambling and even sexual indiscretions. All this results in the family suffering acute embarrassment. It is difficult some times for them to realise that the person concerned is unwell and not plain wicked.

Fortunately effective drugs are now available for the treatment of this condition. This nearly always has to be administered in a psychiatric hospital. The outlook for a person with mania is most favourable today.

LEGAL ASPECTS OF TREATMENT

The vast majority of elderly people requiring in-patient psychiatric treatment are treated on an informal (previously known as "voluntary") basis.

On rare occasions compulsory admission to hospital is required. This would only be if it were in the interests of the person's health or safety or in order to protect other people. The Mental Health Act (1959) is the relevant legislation for England and Wales. The situation in Scotland is covered by the Mental Health (Scotland) Act (1960).

CHAPTER 10

Visitor's Charter

The conduct of any professional person—be he doctor, nurse, minister of religion or social worker—is determined to a large degree by a code of ethics.

The voluntary visitor, in his or her commitment to an old person at home, is in essentially the same situation. Both the professional man and the volunteer have to be aware of their privileged position in having access to an individual's house. Ours is a situation with many responsibilities—and no rights. Above all, the old person's right to privacy, even to the extent of being left alone, should always be respected.

CODE OF CONDUCT

Were an ethical Code of Conduct for Voluntary Visitors ever to be drawn up it might contain the following statements among others:

(1) Helping an elderly frail person is most worthwhile and very rewarding in a personal way. Your interest is likely to be one of the critical factors in determining whether or not such a person can remain at home. A fundamental aim must be to enable the elderly to preserve both their self-respect and their independence.

(2) Remember the importance of good manners. That can ease most difficult or embarrassing situations. Do not be patronising, superior or smug. Avoid making an old person feel an object of pity. Try and be dependable and make your visits on a regular basis.

(3) Your responsibility is primarily to offer friendship and companionship. Most old people appreciate a chat and this means you have to be

a good listener. Never use information received in the course of a visit as a basis for promoting gossip.

(4) Remember, the needs of certain old people are not for conversation. What they want is practical help—with shopping, getting the pension and such like. It's important to be able to differentiate this group of elderly people from those seeking companionship.

(5) Be aware of the various agencies, official and voluntary, in your area responsible for the care and welfare of the elderly. Unless there is consultation from time to time between the various helpers concerned, the old people suffer.

(6) Get to know the name of the old person's family doctor at the outset. Never hesitate to seek help from the doctor, or the other professional people in the community whenever you are concerned about an old person's health or welfare. Do not delay in reporting either a change for the worse in an old person's health or a deterioration in the home circumstances.

(7) Above all, try to be tolerant. Some old people are not easy to visit. They may be crotchety and tactless. They may become forgetful about their personal hygiene. If these constitute real difficulties then, in the interests of everyone, ask for someone else to visit.

Acknowledgements

I would like to acknowledge the advice and support given to me in the preparation of this book by many friends and colleagues, including Mrs. I. Alexander, Marie Black, Ken Blythe, I. A. Cameron, Mima Carlton, Professor Sir William Ferguson Anderson, George Foulkes, Linda Jarvie, Roger M. Jefcoate, Dr. J. F. O. Mitchell, Mary Nicholls, Dr. N. Piercy, Dr. Shirley Piercy, Professor C. I. Phillips, Judith H. Robertson, R. J. M. Smith and D. L. Thom. Mrs. Christine Russell aided by her medical secretarial colleagues typed the manuscript.

I am most grateful to Professor J. N. Anderson for contributing the section on Dental Care. I am indebted to Professor Ivor R. C. Batchelor for his personal introduction to the book and for his help at all stages. Age Concern (Angus) Committee and in particular its Chairman, Mrs. I. McLellan, M.B.E., J.P., have been very supportive.

John Wright and Sons Ltd., have kindly allowed me to quote from the section on Psychiatry and the Law from Frank Fish's *An Outline of Psychiatry* (1964). The Scottish Council of Social Services has given me permission to quote from the passage "Making a will" in their *Handbook of Information in Old People's Welfare in Scotland* (2nd Edition, 1967).

The Health Visitors' Association, 35 Eccleston Square, London SW1V 1PF, has allowed me to reproduce the description of the health visitor's work from their official literature. The extract from the article "Social Work in investigation and management" by Margaret Eden (*Medicine* No. 12, 2nd series 1975 *et seq.*, 560) is reproduced by permission of the publishers, Medical Education (International) Ltd., 73 Wells Street, London W1P 3RD.

Some of the material in Chapter 10 first appeared in an article, "Visitor's Charter for the Elderly", by the author in *New Psychiatry* published by Hospital and Social Services Publications Ltd.

I also wish to thank my father, Dr. James A. Grant Keddie, for reading the proofs.

Montrose, 1978   K.M.G.K.

Chapter Notes

CHAPTER 2

(1) British Red Cross Society, 9 Grosvenor Crescent, London SW1X
7EJ (Tel. 01-235-5454).
    Scottish Branch of the B.R.C.S. is at Alexandra House, 204 Bath
Street, Glasgow G2 4RL (Tel. 041-332-9591).
(2) Women's Royal Voluntary Service, 17 Old Park Lane, London
W1Y 4AJ (Tel. 01-449-6040).
    Scottish Headquarters of the W.R.V.S. is at 19 Grosvenor Crescent,
Edinburgh EH12 5EL (Tel. 031-337-2261).
(3) *Age and Vitality—Commonsense Ways of Adding Life to Your Years*,
Allen & Unwin, London, 1974 (£1.50), by Irene Gore.
(4) The "Gadabout Chair" is available from Selfridges Ltd., P.O. Box
400, London W2 1XP for £6.95 (plus 75p for postage and packing).
(5) The reflective armbands can be obtained from the Royal Society for
the Prevention of Accidents (R.O.S.P.A.), Cannon House, The Priory,
Queensway, Birmingham B4 6BS (Tel. 021-233-2461), for 26p a pair.
(6) The Emer Flash has been approved by R.O.S.P.A. It costs £9.60
and is obtainable from Bush & Meissner Ltd., 275 West End Lane, West
Hampstead, London NW6 1QS.
(7) Contact, 15 Henrietta Street, London WC2 E8QH (Tel. 01-240-
0630).
(8) A comprehensive book of card games, which includes a description
of 20 versions of Patience, is *Hoyle's Modern Encyclopedia of Card Games*,
Robert Hale & Company, London, 1974 (£2.90), by Walter B. Gibson.
(9) *Games You Make and Play*, Macdonald & Janes, London, 1975
(£2.50), by Pia Hsiao, Neil Lorimer and Nick Williams.
(10) The Secretary of Wider Horizons is Miss Vera Dench, 12 Birchwood
Road, London SW17 9BQ.
(11) Friends by Post, 6 Bollin Court, Macclesfield Road, Wilmslow,
Cheshire (Tel. 099-64-27044).
(12) British Correspondence Chess Association, Mr. Brian Clark, Publicity Officer, 17 Cardinal Avenue, Borehamwood, Herts WD6 1EN.

(13) The Wireless for the Bedridden Society, 20 Wimpole Street, London WiM 8BG (Tel. 01-935-0949).

(14) *Holiday addresses in Britain* can be obtained from The Chest and Heart Association, Tavistock House North, London WCiH 9JE, for 50p (postage included). A few nursing homes are listed. Most of the establishments mentioned do not undertake nursing care. Old people who cannot manage easily without help are advised to take someone with them.

(15) The A.A. publication, *Guide for the disabled*, lists hotels, guest houses and farm houses in Britain that cater for the needs of the disabled driver. It is available from the Automobile Association, Fanum House, Leicester Square, London WC2H 7LY for 15p (free to members).

The Central Council for the Disabled, 34 Eccleston Square, London SWiV iPE (Tel. 01-821-1871) has produced an admirable booklet *Holidays for the Physically Handicapped*. It is available for 65p (postage extra). It indicates very clearly the degree of disability that can be reasonably accommodated in any particular establishment. A classification of accommodation is given. This includes those hotels and boarding houses, who for example will take a certain number of incontinent guests and also those where day and night nursing care is available. The guide has a section on overseas holidays. The Central Council for the Disabled advises disabled people always to register with their local branch of the social services department. The department can often given practical assistance by contributing financially to the cost of accommodation and transport. The Council further advise any disabled person going on holiday to take any necessary equipment such as chairs, commodes and rubber sheets and not to rely on hotels to provide these.

Age Concern has published a booklet *Holidays for the Elderly*. This describes those resorts, tour operators and holiday camps offering concessions and reduced party rates for pensioners. It also indicates where special facilities are available for the disabled elderly. The booklet costs 10p (postage extra). For the addresses of Age Concern see (7) of Chapter 7.

(16) Those interested in taking up voluntary work could consult *A Guide to Voluntary Service* by David Hobman (H.M.S.O., 1969). The booklet, *Someone like you can help* (Opportunities for voluntary social service in London) (1971) is available for 18p from The London Council of Social Service, 68 Chalton Street, London NWi iJR.

(17) The Employment Fellowship, Drayton House, Gordon Street, London WC1H 0BE.
Director's office, Allens Green, Sawbridgeworth, Herts (Tel. Bishops Stortford 723012).

(18) *Looking Forward to Retirement*, Ward Lock Ltd., London, 1971 (£2.10), by Keith Mossman.

(19) *A Guide to Activities for Older People*, Elek Books Ltd., London, 1970 (£1.50), by M. Gwyneth Wallis.

(20) The cost (including postage and packing) of having a book sent from Ulverscroft Large Print Books Ltd. is £2.65.

(21) The National Listening Library is at 49 Great Cumberland Place, London W1H 7LH. The reproducer mentioned costs £40. In some cases the social services department will meet the cost, in part or whole. Delivery and servicing are provided free by the National Listening Library. The annual subscription for the cassettes (including postage both ways) is £12. There is no limit to the number hired in a year.

(22) The Royal National Institute for the Blind, 224 Great Portland Street, London W1N 6AA (Tel. 01-388-1266).

(23) Those attending "Nursing for the Family" courses are entitled to purchase a box of Reminder Cards (for approximately 65p). This serves as a "memory bank", whereby a basic nursing procedure can be quickly checked upon.

The British Red Cross Society produces booklets that may be of considerable help in looking after an elderly frail person. One of these is *Home Made Aids for the Disabled* (65p including postage). Another that would be appropriate in certain circumstances is *People in Wheelchairs—Hints for Helpers* (24p including postage). These are both available from the B.R.C.S. Supply Department, 13 Grosvenor Crescent, London SW1X 7EJ.

Another book recommended by the B.R.C.S. for relatives caring for a disabled person is *Handling the Handicapped* (produced by the Chartered Society of Physiotherapy). This is available from the publisher, Woodhead Faulkner Ltd., 7 Rose Crescent, Cambridge CB2 3LL, for £1.95 (25p extra for post and packaging) or from book shops.

(24) The National Council for the Single Woman and her Dependants, 166 Victoria Street, London SW1 5BR (Tel. 01-828-5511).

CHAPTER 3

(1)   *Easy Cooking for One or Two*, Penguin 1972 (40p), by Louise Davies.
(2)   Details of the slide kits can be obtained from Miss Louise Davies, Head of the Geriatric Nutrition Unit, Queen Elizabeth College, University of London, Atkins Building, Campden Hill, London W8 7AH.
(3)   The W.R.V.S. recipe leaflets are available for a penny each from W.R.V.S., 17 Old Park Lane, London W1Y 4AJ.
(4)   (a) *All about Home Heating*, Argus Books Ltd., 1975 (£1.50), by R. H. Warring.
      (b) *Keeping Warm for Half the Cost* costs £1.25 (including post and packaging) and is available from J. A. Colesby and P. J. Townsend, 151 Leicester Road, Mountsorrel, Leicestershire LE12 7DB.
(5)   If an elderly person, who is not getting supplementary benefit, appears to need financial help because of exceptional heating costs, he should be advised to consider claiming for the supplementary benefit. Leaflet SB 1, which includes a claim form, is available from a Post Office or the local Social Security office.
      The weekly supplementary benefit is intended to cover a person's normal spending on heating. In certain exceptional circumstances—poor health, restricted mobility, need for a new heater or a draughty and damp house—an additional special heating allowance may be claimed for. The leaflet, OC 2, *Supplementary benefits: help with heating costs* (available from the local Social Security office) explains the system.
(6)   The leaflet, *Warm up for the Winter*, is available from Age Concern, Bernard Sunley House, 60 Pitcairn Road, Mitcham, Surrey CR4 3LL, for 5p (postage extra).
(7)   In this context the leaflet *The right to fuel* is worth reading. It is available from The British Association of Settlements, 7 Exton Street, London SE1 for 25p.
(8)   Details of hobs, ovens and grills using Calor Gas can be obtained by writing to Domestic Appliance Adviser Calor Gas, Windsor Road, Slough, Berks SL1 2EQ.
(9)   The tape and slides on "Hypothermia in the Elderly" can be hired for a period of up to 28 days from the Medical Recording Service Foundation, Kitts Croft, Writtle, Chelmsford CM1 3EH, for £2 (V.A.T. is extra).
(10) Mr. A. R. Noble, Promotion Manager, Dreamland Appliances,

Hythe, Southampton, will send details of their electric underblankets to anyone interested.

(11) Full details of the aluminium foil reflector screen can be obtained from the Hon. Brenda Carter, Wakeham, Rogate, near Petersfield, Hants.

(12) These helpful observations are from the April 1974 issue of *Which?* which examined the range of electric kettles available on the market at that time.

(13) The following are *Directions for Use* with the Russell Hobbs Electric Kettle for an old person who is a little forgetful:

   (1) Fill kettle with water to V mark.

      Water can be hot or cold.

   (2) Fit socket into kettle.

   (3) Insert plug into walls.

   (4) Switch on at wall.

      Hands should be dry!

   (5) Push in red disc on kettle.

   (6) After 3 minutes: Kettle boils and red disc clicks out.

   (7) Switch off at wall.

      Hands should be dry again!

   (8) Disconnect socket from kettle.

   (9) Now pour—carefully!

An elderly person should be warned of the dangers of filling an electric kettle while it is still connected to the mains. In the presence of an electric fault, the user is liable to get a severe shock.

(14) (a) The Sieger Boy Can Opener can be operated one handed, providing the can is adequately stabilised, i.e. by wedging it in a drawer. The retail price is approximately 85p and it is available from M. Gilbert, 1109 Greenford Road, Greenford, Middlesex.

   (b) A wall can opener, suitable also for those with arthritis, can be obtained from Rentoul Workshops, Royal Cornhill Hospital (City) Truro, Cornwall, for £3.50 plus 8% V.A.T.

(15) The Disabled Living Foundation Aids Centre, 346 Kensington High Street, London W14 8NS (Tel. 01-602-2491).

A range of stainless steel cutlery, "Sunflower Selecta" Grip Cutlery has been designed specifically for people with a disability of hard, arm or shoulder which restricts the ability to grip ordinary kitchen utensils. There are five different spoons, a knife and a fork (costing between 57p and 93p) and three easily interchangeable plastic grips (costing 27p) (1975 prices). The cutlery is available from The Disabled Living Foundation Aids Centre.

The Foundation has a useful publication for the elderly and/or disabled, *Kitchen Sense*, costing £1.75 (including postage).

(16) Homecraft Supplies Ltd., 27 Trinity Road, London SW17 2SF, will supply non-slip bath mats from 95p to £1.16. Plastic covered bath-boards and plastic covered cork seats are also available.

A range of bathing aids can also be obtained under the trade name "Sunflower", from F. Llewellyn and Co. Ltd., South East Princes, St. Nicholas Place, Liverpool L30 0AA. They produce, for example, a moulded Shallowbath which fits over the bath and allows for easy entry and exit. Such equipment is strong and also comfortable to use, being warm to the touch. The cost of Shallowbath is £36.50 (carriage and V.A.T. are extra).

(17) The McCullagh Commode Chair is available from Chas. F. Thachray Ltd., St. Anthony's Road, Leeds LS11 8DT. The cost for the commode, without bedpan, is £28, including carriage but exclusive of V.A.T. (March 1975 quotation).

(18) The Rippling Bed and pump are available from Gelman Hawsley Ltd., 12 Peter Road, Lancing, Sussex, and cost £53, exclusive of post and packing and V.A.T. (June 1975 quotation).

(19) The booklet *Hoists and Walking Aids*, is available from Equipment for the Disabled, 2 Foredown Drive, Portslade, Sussex BN4 2BD, for £1.71 (including postage).

Mecanaids Ltd., St. Catherine Street, Gloucester GL1 2BX, produce a range of hoists designed to help the elderly and the disabled with the problems of lifting and bathing.

(20) *Which?* magazine, in its *Money Which?* issue, September, 1974, produced a most valuable Social Security check list. This is a quick guide to the forty-two ways in which the State helps people financially.

Age Concern (Bernard Sunley House, 60 Pitcairn Road, Mitcham, Surrey) has produced for 20p a booklet *Money Guide . . . notes for the retired on pensions, taxes allowances, concessions and savings.*

This organisation has also published *Your Rights* for 15p plus 10p forwarding charge. This details all the welfare benefits to which old age pensioners are entitled.

(21) The amount that old age pensioners can earn, before their pensions are affected, is at present (April 1977) £50. All income is of course subject to the usual tax regulations. Tax has to be paid where income, over and above a full state retirement pension, exceeds about £6 a week for single people over 65, about £8.50 for married men and about £2.70 for single women under 65. Earnings do not affect the amount of the pension after the age of 70.

(22) The pamphlet *How to outwit the bogus "officials" who trick householders*, is worth having and is available free from The Local Government Information Office for England and Wales, 36 Old Queen Street, Westminster, London SW1H 9HZ.

(23) There is a booklet available which gives guidance on the legal and technical problems faced by people with debt problems. This is *Debt counselling* by John Blamire and Arthur Izzard. It can be obtained from the Birmingham Settlement Money Advice Centre, 318 Summer Lane, Birmingham 19, for 85p plus 11p postage and packing.

(24) Information on legal aid can be obtained from the following addresses: The Law Society, 113 Chancery Lane, London WC2A 1PL (for legal aid provisions in England and Wales).

The Law Society of Scotland, Legal Aid Central Committee, 27 Drumsheugh Gardens, Edinburgh EH3 7YR.

The Incorporated Law Society of Northern Ireland, Legal Aid Department, Law Courts Building, Chichester Street, Belfast BT1 3JZ.

Each of these Societies has produced a free explanatory guide to legal aid, which is worth sending for. The names of solicitors on legal aid panels can be obtained from the nearest office of the Citizens' Advice Bureau or by counsulting the yellow pages of the telephone directory.

(25) An excellent booklet *Practical Problems after a Death* has been published by National Association of Citizens' Advice Bureaux, 26 Bedford Square, London WC1 3HU. It is available free. A Scottish edition has been produced by the Scottish Citizens' Advice Bureaux Committee, 18/19 Claremont Crescent, Edinburgh EH7 4QD.

What to do when someone dies is a *Which?* publication and is available from Consumers' Association, Subscription Department, Caxton Hill, Hertford SG13 7LZ, for £1.25.

(26) Pharos Assurance Friendly Society, Woodcut House, Ashford Road, Hollingbourne, Maidstone, Kent ME17 1XH.

CHAPTER 4

(1) The Royal Society for the Prevention of Accidents (Cannon House, The Priory, Queensway, Birmingham B4 6BS) (Tel. 021-233-2461) has produced two excellent booklets on the prevention of falls, fires and other mishaps in the home. *Safety in Retirement* (20p) and *Stop Accidents in the Home* (24p) (postage included) are available from R.O.S.P.A. and are good value for money. *Safety in Retirement* is of particular relevance where an elderly person is about to move into another house. By working through the Basic Safety Check List in this booklet, any householder can rapidly discover the weak points in a home.

The Fire Protection Association, Aldermary House, Queen Street, London EC4, is actively concerned about the prevention of fires in homes occupied by the elderly. The Association would send appropriate publicity literature on request. The Home Office publication, *Danger from fire: how to protect your home*, is very comprehensive and it highlights the particular fire risks facing old people. This booklet can be obtained free from the Fire Protection Association.

(2) It is usually necessary for a house to be rewired after 25 years where rubber-sheathed cables were used originally. The Electrical Contractors' Association, 55 Catherine Place, Westminster, London SW1E 6ET (Tel. 01-828-2932) will undertake a free safety check of wiring and installation in homes in any part of the U.K., except Scotland.

(3) Homesaver Fire Blankets can be obtained from Homesaver Fire Appliances, P.O. Box 39, Cheltenham, Glos. (Tel. 0242-57414). The 3′ × 3′ and the 4′ × 4′ blankets cost £2.20 and £4.00 respectively (V.A.T. extra 8%) (price quoted April 1975).

(4) Talking of labour saving tools for the garden, I am very impressed with the Swoe, a recent and most versatile invention. This is really two tools in one, having blades on three sides, which enables one to work, for example, all round a plant without moving. It costs £6.46 (including V.A.T.—April 1975 quotation) and is made by Wilkinson Sword Ltd., Totteridge Road, High Wycombe, Bucks HP1 6EG.

(5) *The Easy Path to Gardening* is a very readable book which encourages older people to continue enjoying gardening as a hobby. It costs £1.25 and is published by Reader's Digest Association Ltd., 25 Berkley Square, London W1X 6AB.

(6) Anyone considering applying for a grant should contact the local branch of the Department of Environment. This Department (2 Marsham Street, London SW1 P3EB) has produced a helpful booklet on the subject, *Your guide to house renovation grants*. The Scottish Development Department, 80 Princes Street, Edinburgh EH2 2HH, will provide on request, *Improve Your Home—Grants Available*. Both these publications are issued free of charge. Local authorities can, if they choose, grant above average rent rebates and rent allowances for disabled people. These allowances would then continue on a regular basis. The regulations are explained in a booklet, *Housing Grants and Allowances for Disabled People*. This is available from the Housing Department, Central Council for the Disabled, 34 Eccleston Square, London SW1, for 25p; the information in this booklet applies only to England and Wales.

(7) A dog licence is renewable each year for 37½p.

(8) The National Canine Defence League, 10 Seymour Street, Portman Square, London W1H 5WB (Tel. 01-935-5511).

(9) The Royal Society for the Prevention of Cruelty to Animals, The Manor House, Horsham, Sussex RH12 1HG (Tel. 0403-64181).

(10) The Scottish Society for the Prevention of Cruelty to Animals, 19 Melville Street, Edinburgh EH3 7PL (Tel. 031-225-6418).

(11) The Dog Aid Society of Scotland Ltd., 2 Ainslie Place, Edinburgh EA3 6AR (Tel. 031-225-7570).

(12) The Companionship Trust, 58 Broadwalk, South Woodford, London E18 (Tel. 01-989-4130).

(13) The Royal Society for the Protection of Birds, The Lodge, Sandy, Bedfordshire SG19 2DL (Tel. Sandy 80551).

(14) *The New Birds Table*, David & Charles, Newton Abbot, 1973 (£2.20), by Tony Soper.

(15) The Wildfowl Trust, Slimbridge, Gloucester GL2 7BT, will send details of the "Adopt a Duck" scheme to anyone interested. There are also Swan and Barnacle Goose Supporters Schemes.

(16) Mr. Peter Wilson of Tackbrook Tropicals, 244 Vauxhall Bridge Road, London SW1, would send information booklets on fish keeping on request. *How to enjoy being an Aquarist* by Keith Barraclough and Gordon Holmes is available from Tackbrook Tropicals for 33½p (postage included).

(17) The Disabled Drivers' Association (D.D.A.), Ashwellthorpe, Norwich NR16 1EX (Tel. Fundenhall 499), aims to assist all seriously disabled

people towards a fuller life through greater mobility. The Association will, for example, advise any individual who is having difficulties claiming for the new mobility allowance introduced in 1976. Disabled people entitled to a retirement pension (60 for a woman, 65 for a man) are not eligible for the mobility allowance. The allowance will eventually be paid to every severely disabled person, aged 5 or over but under pension age, who is unable or virtually unable to walk. Initially people in the 15 to 25 age group could claim. The scheme was then gradually extended to the other age groups.

The following publication might be of interest to disabled drivers and their relatives: *Wheel Chairs and Outdoor Transport*, available for £1.71 (including postage) from Equipment for the Disabled, 2 Foredown Drive, Portslade, Sussex BN4 2BB.

(18) For Age Concern addresses see (7) of Chapter 7.

CHAPTER 5

(1) Surveys have confirmed the high incidence of illness in the elderly.

A report published by the U.S. Department of Health showed that in the United States of America of every 100 persons over 65 years of age interviewed, 33 suffered from arthritis, 17 from heart conditions, 16 from high blood pressure, 12 from gastro-intestinal disease, 10 from a mental disorder, 5 from diabetes, 4 from asthma, 3 from chronic bronchitis and 2 from thyroid disease. (This information is from *Task Force on Prescription Drugs, U.S. Department H.E.W.: The Drug Users* Washington, D.C., Government Printing Office (1968).)

A similar pattern of illness in the elderly is likely to be found in the United Kingdom, apart from a higher incidence of chronic bronchitis.

(2) The Family Doctor Booklet series includes *Sleeping and Not Sleeping* by Ian Oswald. This is a reassuring publication, which helps to correct many of the popular misconceptions held about the nature of, and the need for, sleep. It is available from the British Medical Association, Family Doctor House, 47–51 Chalton Street, London NW1 1HT, for 25p (package/postage an extra 8p).

(3) The Disabled Living Foundation Aids Centre, 346 Kensington High Street, London W14 8NS (Tel. 01-602-2491).

The Scottish Information Services for the Disabled, 18/19 Claremont Crescent, Edinburgh EH7 4QD (Tel. 031-556-3882).

Pifco Ltd., Failsworth, Manchester M35 0HS, make an excellent range of illuminated magnifiers. One such magnifier with a $3\frac{1}{4}$ inch diameter lens costs £1.95 (plus 95p for postage and packing).

(4) The Royal National Institute for the Blind, 224 Great Portland Street, London W1N 6AA (Tel. 01-388-1266).

(5) The Guide Dogs for the Blind Association, 113 Uxbridge Road, Ealing, London W5 (Tel. 01-567-7001).

(6) Details of N.O.D. can be obtained by writing to M.R.C. Blind Mobility Research Unit, Department of Psychology, Nottingham University, University Park, Nottingham NG7 2RD.

(7) *In Touch—aids and services for blind and partially sighted people,* British Broadcasting Corporation, London, 1973 (60p).

(8) The Scottish Home and Health Department have recently produced a free booklet, *General Guidance to Hearing Aid Users.* This is very easy to read and is worth sending for from the Department at St. Andrews House, Edinburgh EH1 3DE.

(9) The booklet *Hearing Aids,* costs 10p and is available from The Royal National Institute for the Deaf, 105 Gower Street, London WC1E 6AH. This gives an objective account of the instruments available.

(10) These are examples of portable communicators:

(a) A. & M. Communicator comprises an earphone of the lorgnette type and a microphone. It costs £28 and is manufactured by A. & M. Hearing Aids Ltd. Kelvin Way, Crawley, Sussex.

(b) Leyton Instrument Co. Ltd., (163 Oxford Road, Reading RC1 7XP) has marketed the Linco Converser Geriatric Aural Aid, mainly for use in welfare homes and geriatric hospitals. The instrument consists of a microphone, an amplifier and a head set with a pair of earphones. It is portable (carrying bag provided) and weighs only 5 lb. The instrument can even be connected to a radio, tape-recorder or gramophone pick-up. The cost (including V.A.T.) for the instrument and the carrying bag is £78.57.

(11) The magazine *Hearing* is available from the Royal National Institute for the Deaf (for address see (9) above) for £1 a year post free.

(12) The British Association of the Hard of Hearing, Briarfield, Syke Ings, Iver, Bucks.

(13) The Society of Chiropodists, 8 Wimpole Street, London W1M 8BX (Tel. 01-580-3227).

The Institute of Chiropodists, 59 Gloucester Place, London W1H 3PE (Tel. 01-935-6874).

(14) The Chest and Heart Association is at the following addresses:
Tavistock House North, Tavistock Square, London WC1H 9JE (Tel. 01-387-3012).

65 Castle Street, Edinburgh EH2 3LT (Tel. 031-225-6527).

28 Bedford Street, Belfast BT2 7FJ (Tel. 0232-20184).

The Association has produced two leaflets that are particularly worth sending for. These are *Stroke Illness—twenty questions and the answers* and *Learning to Speak Again—hints for the patient's family and friends.*

A series of seven cassettes with accompanying visual aids and leaflets for helpers has been produced by the Association as a project, *Learning to Speak Again after a Stroke.* The cassettes are only to be used under the guidance of a speech therapist. The cost is £24 (including postage and packing).

(15) Valerie Eaton Griffith has been a pioneer in the movement to use volunteers in the rehabilitation of stroke patients. Her article, "Volunteer Scheme for Dysphasia and Allied Problems in Stroke Patients", was published in the 13th September 1975 edition of the *British Medical Journal.*

Miss Griffith has also described her contribution to the recovery from a stroke of Patricia Neal, the film star, in a very moving and also practical book. This is *A Stroke in the Family*, Wildwood House, London, 1975 (£1.50).

(16) *Stroke—A Diary of Recovery*, Faber & Faber, London (1966), by Douglas Ritchie.

(17) The various pick-up sticks are listed in Comparative Test Report Number 8 of The National Fund for Research into Crippling Diseases, Vincent House, 1 Springfield Road, Horsham, Sussex.

(18) The Electricity Council, 30 Millbank, London SW1P 4RD.

(19) Haven Products Ltd., 24 George Square, Glasgow G2 1EG, has recently marketed a versatile type of walking trolley, called the Trolley-Aid. This can be fitted with one of three different types of walking support, all interchangeable and independently adjustable—walking stick handles, a horizontal bar or fore-arm trough crutches. The Trolley-Aid has a top

tray with a wipe clean surface for the carrying of meals and such like. There is a lower tray at a convenient height for easy access from a sitting position. The price (January 1976) for the Trolley-Aid is £30 (the item is zero rated).

Details of other walking-aid trolleys are to be found in No. 8 in the series, *Equipment for the Disabled*, obtainable from the National Fund for Research into Crippling Diseases, Vincent House, 1 Springfield Road, Horsham, Sussex, for £1.05 (postage extra).

(20) *Coping with Disablement* is available from Consumers' Association, Subscription Department, Caxton Hill, Hertford SG13 7LZ, for £1.50 (including postage).

(21) *Aids for the Severely Handicapped*, Sector Publishing, 1974 (£4.20), edited by Keith Copeland.

(22) The Disablement Income Group, Queens House, 180–182A Tottenham Court Road, London W1P 0BD (Tel. 01-636-1946).

D.I.G. Scotland, 3 Howe Street, Edinburgh EH3 6TE (Tel. 031-556-9406).

(23) Gelling Pads are particularly helpful for women. Details from Gelulose Incontinence Products Ltd., 16 Dolphin Street, Ardwick Green, Manchester M12 6BG.

(24) Information on Kanga Pants can be obtained from Kanga Hospital Products Ltd., P.O. Box 39, Spring Side Mill, Belmont Road, Bromley Cross, Bolton BL7 9QN.

(25) A book on altering garments for incontinent patients can be obtained from the Disabled Living Foundation, 346 Kensington High Street, London W14 8NS, for 80p.

The title is *Incontinence—some problems, suggestions and conclusions*.

The Foundation also has information lists on *Clothing and Incontinence*, *Notes on Odour Control* and *Clothing for Handicapped Adults* and will send these on request.

CHAPTER 6

(1) The results of the Hull Study on telephones were published in 1973 as No. 53 in a series *Occupational Papers on Social Administration*, G. Bell and Sons (£1.75 paperback).

(2)   The rental for a standard table telephone is £8.91, and £7.83 for a shared line. It costs 43p per quarter to rent an amplifying hand-set. This has a volume control on the earpiece and is of assistance to the hard of hearing. Where an old person speaks quietly a faint speech amplifier can be rented. This costs £1.35 a quarter, after a connection charge of £3.24. (All prices are accurate for February 1976.)

(3)   Interlock Systems for the Disabled, Sherrards Training Centre for Spastics, Digswell Hill, Old Welwyn, Herts., manufacture the "Intercom Door-lock" kit for a basic cost of £42. Where the equipment has not been prescribed by a doctor, V.A.T. at 25% has to be paid in addition.

(4)   See (3) of Chapter 5.

(5)   The Alex Personal Alarm can be obtained from Rowat & Co. Ltd., 30 City Road, London EC1Y 2BA, for £1 (including postage). The Institute for Consumer Ergonomics Ltd. (University of Technology, Loughborough, Leicestershire LE11 3TU) recently completed an evaluation of alarm systems for the National Corporation for the Care of Old People. The report, *Alarm Systems for Elderly and Disabled People*, is available for £1. The study demonstrates the importance of efficient but simply operated systems. Unfortunately, the report indicates that many of the aids tested had drawbacks.

(6)   The address of Davis Safety Controls is Brunswick Industrial Estate, Newcastle upon Tyne NE13 7BA. Their "Homecall" system costs £3 per week. This price excludes payment to the warden who will normally be employed by the local authority.

(7)   Cass Electronics Ltd., Crabtree Road, Thorpe, Surrey TW20 8RN will send details on request of the Cass Community Care Alarm Systems.

CHAPTER 7

(1)   A penetrating analysis of the contribution family doctors could, and perhaps should, make to the health care of old people was set out in *No one to blame?* (*A searching enquiry into the role of the G.P. and the elderly patient*), published in 1976 by Help the Aged, 8 Denholm Street, London W1A 2AP. It is available free.

(2)   The national body responsible for health visitors is The Health

Visitors' Association, 36 Eccleston Square, London SW1 (Tel. 01-834-9523).

The Health visitor is a nurse with a post-registration qualification, who provides a continuing service to families and individuals in the community. The Council for the Education and Training of Health Visitors describes the main parts of a health visitor's work as follows: (a) The prevention of mental, physical and emotional ill health and its consequences. (b) Early detection of ill health and the surveillance of high risk groups. (c) Recognition and identification of need and mobilisation of appropriate resources. (d) Health teaching. (e) Provision of care; this includes support during periods of stress.

(3) The national body responsible for district nurses is The Queen's Nursing Institute, 57 Lower Belgrave Street, London SW1W oLR (Tel. 01-730-0355).

(4) Further information about the part played by the remedial professions in the care of elderly people living at home can be obtained by writing to the following addresses:

The British Association of Occupational Therapists, 20 Rede Place, Bayswater, London W2 4TU (Tel. 01-229-9738/9).

The British Dietetic Association, 305 Daimler House, Paradise Street, Birmingham B12 BJ (Tel. 021-643-5483).

The College of Speech Therapists, 47 St. John's Wood High Street, London NW8 7NJ (Tel. 01-586-1958).

The Chartered Society of Physiotherapy, 14 Bedford Row, London WC1R 4ED (Tel. 01-242-1941/6).

(5) The national organisation responsible for qualified social workers is the British Association of Social Workers (B.A.S.W.), 16 Kent Street, Birmingham B5 6RD (Tel. 012-622-3911). The Scottish office is at 50 Queen Street, Edinburgh EH2 3NS (Tel. 031-226-4526).

Margaret Eden, in an article addressed to doctors ("Social work in investigation and management" in *Medicine* No. 12, 2nd series 1975 *et seq.*), describes the various types of contribution a social worker can make to the care of a patient and his family. It is suggested that a social worker can often be helpfully involved in the following situations: (a) Overt social problems and material needs and the provision or coordination of services for these. (b) The family of a patient needing practical help or support, e.g. a sick or handicapped patient living at home, a depressed mother with small children. (c) Patients and/or families with anxieties, fears and distress about illness, handicap, crippling disease, terminal illness. (d) Marital, parental and family problems. (e) People particularly at risk for identifiable reasons (through loss, bereavement, loss of role, loss of function; through need to change life pattern; through recurrent or progressive illness; through their social situation, e.g. living alone; through their condition, e.g. elderly, schizophrenic, alcoholic). (f) Patients whose condition is not explainable in terms of their physical or psychiatric condition, who relapse inexplicably, or have exhausted treatment possibilities. (g) Repeated small complaints, vague psychosomatic symptoms. (h) Suicidal attempt. (i) Non-accidental injury to children.

(6) See (16) of Chapter 2.

(7) Age Concern England, National Old People's Welfare Council, Bernard Sunley House, 60 Pitcairn Road, Mitcham, Surrey CR4 3LL (Tel. 01-640-5431).

Age Concern Scotland, Scottish Old People's Welfare Council, 5 Manor Place, Edinburgh EH3 7DH (Tel. 031-255-5000/1).

Age Concern Wales, National Council for the Elderly in Wales, 47 Butleigh Avenue, Llandaff, Cardiff (Tel. 0222-44141).

Age Concern Northern Ireland, 2 Annadale Avenue, Belfast 7 (Tel. Belfast 643886).

(8) See (1) of Chapter 2.

(9) See (2) of Chapter 2.

(10) National Citizens' Advice Bureaux Council, 26 Bedford Square, London WC1B 3HU (Tel. 01-636-4006).

The Scottish Association of Citizens' Advice Bureaux is at 12 Queen Street, Edinburgh EH2 1JE (Tel. 031-225-5323).

(11) The addresses of the National Councils of Social Service are as follows:

The National Council of Social Service, 26 Bedford Square, London WC1B 3HU (Tel. 01-636-4066).

Scottish Council of Social Service, 18/19 Claremont Crescent, Edinburgh EH7 4HX (Tel. 031-556-3882).

Council of Social Service for Wales, 2 Cathedral Road, Cardiff CF1 9XR (Tel. 0222-21456).

Northern Ireland Council of Social Service, 2 Annandale Avenue, Belfast BT7 3JH (Tel. 643886/645489).

CHAPTER 8

(1) Pre-Retirement Association, 19 Undine Street, Tooting, London SW17 8PP (Tel. 01-767-3225/6).

The Association has recently produced an audio-visual package course, *The Next 20 Years*, suitable for pre-retirement course organisers. It comprises eight tape/slide programmes and leaflets covering all aspects of Preparation for Retirement. Cassette tape recordings are by Richard Baker. The Pre-Retirement Association will send details on request.

(2) *The Retirement Book*, Hamish Hamilton Ltd., London, 1974 (£2.75), ed. by Michael Pilch.

(3) The British Pensioners and Trade Union Action Committee, 138 Stoke Road, Slough, Berks. SLZ 5AS.

The Scottish Old Age Pensioners Association, 12 Gordon Street, Lochgelly, Fife.

(4) The British Association of Retired Persons, 14 Frederick Street, Edinburgh EH2 2HB (Tel. 031-225-7334).

(5) National Federation of Old Age Pensions Associations, "Melling House", 91 Preston New Road, Blackburn, Lancs. (Tel. Blackburn 52606).

The weekly paper, *Pensioners' Voice*, costs 3p.

(6) Help the Aged, P.O. Box 30, London N1 1RF (Tel. 01-359-6318), constantly needs funds in order to continue distributing its newspaper *Yours*.

The annual donation for *Yours* is £3 (including postage).

(7) Mrs. Evie Spector of Age Concern, Lewisham, has vividly described the particular pensioners' self-help movement, with which she has been associated. This is available in a report of a conference *Self-Help, Participation and the Elderly*, held at Southampton University in September 1974. This report can be obtained from the Department of Sociology and Social Administration, at the University, for £1.

(8) Cruse Clubs, 126 Sheen Road, Richmond, Surrey (Tel. 01-940-4818).

(9) The National Association of Widows, 65 Eastgate Street, Stafford.

(10) *Grief: and how to live with it*, Allen & Unwin, London, 1971 (£1.50), by Sarah Morris.

(11) The regulations that are laid down in relation to the number of

persons who may occupy a Council house vary with each local authority. As a broad guide, I quote here from the regulations of one particular local authority in Scotland:

"Separate bedrooms required for—

(a) Husband and wife;

(b) One or two children under 10 years of age;

(c) One or two persons of the same sex under 60 years of age;

(d) A person whom the Medical Officer considers should sleep in a room alone;

(e) One or two individuals of the same sex, 60 years of age, or over, accepted by the Council as forming part of the applicant's family for the purpose of housing.

N.B. In assessing the household circumstances the living-room shall be disregarded."

(12) The Abbeyfield Society Ltd., 35A High Street, Potters Bar, Herts (Tel. Potters Bar 43371).

(13) Anchor Housing Association (formerly Help the Aged Housing Association), Oxenford House, Magdalen Street, Oxford (Tel. Oxford 22261).

(14) The National Federation of Housing Societies, 86 Strand, London WC2R 0EG (Tel. 01-836-2741).

Further Reading

GENERAL

The Psychology of Human Ageing, Pelican, 1966 (30p), by D. B. Bromley. An excellent introduction to the understanding of the problems of the old.

Human Relations in Old Age (A handbook for Health Visitors, Social Workers and others), Faber & Faber, London, 1967 (£1.30), by T. N. Rudd. This book contains a lot of material of relevance to the lay public as well as professionals.

Old Age: Themes, Routledge & Kegan Paul, London, 1972 (£1.25 cloth, 60p limp), ed. by Edward H. Jones, Michael Hayhoe & Beryl Jones. This is a collection of prose, poetry and short stories from writers, past and present, from all over the world. Basically intended for secondary school children, it should appeal to anyone involved in helping the old.

Common Human Needs, Allen & Unwin, London, 1973 (£1.65), by Charlotte Towle.

Discussion Topics for Oldsters in Nursing Homes: 365 Things to Talk About, Charles C. Thomas, Publishers, Illinois, 1974 ($11.75), by Toni Merrill.

Why Survive? Being Old in America, Harper & Row, New York, 1975 ($15.00), by Robert N. Butler.

The Best Years of Your Life: A guide to the Art and Science of Ageing, Atheneum Publishers, New York, 1975 ($10.00), by L. Bellak.

Loneliness, Maurice Temple Smith, 1975 (£1.25 paperback), by Jeremy Scabrook. This book is movingly illustrated and attempts to show what it is like to be lonely—and lonely all the time.

Helping the Elderly, Age Concern Wales bilingual booklet. Available for 35p (post free) from Age Concern, Bernard Sunley House, 60 Pitcairn Road, Mitcham, Surrey.

Care of the Dying, Priory Press, London, 1975 (£2.50), by Richard Lamerton. This is a sensitive and practical book written for relatives, doctors and nurses caring for a terminally ill patient.

HEALTH

Services for Mental Illness related to Old Age, H.M.S.O., 1972, by the Department of Health and Social Security.

Care of the Aged, Priory Press Ltd., London, 1972 (£2.25), by Dennis Hyams.

Caring for the Elderly, William Heinemann Medical Books, London, 1973 (90p), by Gladys Francis.

Aging and Mental Health (Positive Psychosocial Approaches), The C.V. Mosby Company, U.S.A., 1973, (£3.30), by Robert N. Butler and Myrna I. Lewis.

Psychogeriatrics—An Introduction to the Psychiatry of Old Age, Churchill Livingstone, Edinburgh, 1974 (£2.25), by Brice Pitt.

Health for Old Age and *Arrangements for Old Age*. These are *Which?* guides (75p each) available from Consumers' Association, Caxton Hill, Hertford SG13 7LZ. Most helpful and practical.

The booklets, *Your Home and Your Rheumatism* and *Your Garden and Your Rheumatism*, are available for 10p each from The Arthritis and Rheumatism Council, Faraday House, Charing Cross Road, London WC2H 0HN.

THE DISABLED

Help Yourselves: Handbook for Hemiplegics and their Families, Butterworths, London, 1972, 2nd Edition (75p), by P. E. Jay *et al.*

The National Fund for Research into Crippling Diseases, 1 Springfield Road, Horsham, Sussex, has published an illuminating series, *Comparative Test Reports* (Refrigerators, Reading Aids/Page Turners, Prismatic Spectacles, Easy Chairs, Cookers, Gas Fires, Pick-up Sticks, Can Openers, Vacuum Cleaners, Food Mixers and Bath Aids). Equipment for the Disabled booklets (Wheelchairs and Outside Transport, Communications, Clothing and Dressing, Home Management, Personal Care, Gardening and Leisure, Housing and Furniture and Hoists and Walking Aids) are available from Equipment for the Disabled, 2 Foredown Drive, Portslade, Sussex.

ABC of Services and General Information for Disabled People by Barbara Macmorland. Available from Disablement Income Group, Queens House, 180–182A Tottenham Court Road, London W1P 0BD, for 37p (including postage). An excellent publication—most comprehensive.

WELFARE STATE

Consumer's Guide to the British Social Services, Penguin Books, 3rd Edition, 1973 (50p) by Phyllis Willmott.

Family Benefits and Pensions, published by Department of Health and Social Security.

Help for Handicapped People, prepared by Department of Health and Social Security and The Welsh Office. *Help for Handicapped People in Scotland*, prepared by the Scottish Office.

RETIREMENT

On Your Own, Tom Stacey Ltd., London, 1971 (£1.25), by George Howard.

Enjoy Your Retirement, David & Charles, Newton Abbot, 1973 (£1.95), by Tom Griffiths.

A Lively Retirement, Queen Anne Press, London, 1975 (£1.30), ed. by William Loving. This includes a useful chapter on finance.

Thinking about Retirement, Pergamon Press, Oxford, 1975 (£2.55), by J. H. Wallis.

Useful Local Addresses

You are invited to fill in the relevant information for your own locality.

Family Doctors

District Nurses and Health Visitors

Ministers of Religion

Department of Health and Social Security

Department of Social Work

Social Workers

Chemists

Chiropodists

Red Cross

Hospitals

Home Help Service

Meals-on-Wheels

Women's Royal Voluntary Service

Nursing Equipment

Handicapped Aids

Luncheon Clubs

Pensioners' Clubs

Post Office

Rotary

Round Table

Veterinary Surgeon

Other Addresses

List of People being Visited

Names	Addresses	Comments

Appendix[1]

Throughout this book, reference is made to individuals, groups, and organizations serving the elderly of Britain. The purpose of this Appendix is to supplement Keddie's book by providing information about the kinds of services available to elderly Americans. In the United States the number of persons over 65 has increased greatly in recent years. There are now approximately 22 million people, or more than one in ten Americans, over age 65. As in England and other countries, there are community, state, and national programs designed to meet the social and medical needs of the elderly.

In the United States most of the federal efforts on behalf of the elderly, other than social security, old age assistance, and medicare, were established by the Older Americans Act of 1965 and the Economic Opportunity Act of 1964. The social needs of the elderly were the focus of these programs and, as a result, there has been much needed growth in the scope and benefits of national programs. The Older Americans Act created the Administration on Aging (AOA), which is part of the U.S. Department of Health, Education, and Welfare. The primary responsibility of this agency is to administer community service programs for states and one example of its work has been the establishment of numerous senior citizen centers throughout the country. Foster Grandparent programs (discussed below), information referral centers, and Retired Senior Volunteer programs have also been sponsored by the Administration on Aging. Dr. Arthur S. Flemming is currently the head of this organization.

Some of the programs established by AOA are now self-sufficient or managed by other administrative agencies at a local or state level. The following is a description of services that would probably exist in a medium-sized (150,000–200,000 persons) city and metropolitan area in the United States.

[1]Prepared by Dr. William J. Hoyer, Department of Psychology, 331 Huntington Hall, Syracuse University, Syracuse, New York 13210, USA.

ACCORD (Action Coalition to Create Opportunities for Retirement with Dignity)

ACCORD offers opportunities for those individuals over 65 to become actively involved in many community projects. ACCORD operates a senior citizen discount program which gives elderly 10% discounts on public transportation, at some entertainment events, and at participating stores.

CALL-A-BUS Service

This is a door-to-door bus program for those who find it difficult or impossible to use public transportation. There is a nominal charge (50 cents) for the service. There are usually other organizations and community programs that offer emergency transportation for elderly shut-ins.

FOSTER GRANDPARENT PROGRAM

This is an opportunity for low income elderly to work with children who have special needs. Typically, the older person visits a local facility for developmentally-disabled children, and a warm, trusting one-on-one helping relationship is established between the older person and the child.

The Foster Grandparent Program now has approximately 10,500 volunteers working at 137 different institutions in all 50 states. The volunteers to be eligible must be over age 60 and earn less than $2000 per year. The Foster Grandparents are paid $1670 per year for 20 hours per week of work and they are reimbursed for their transportation costs. Each Foster Grandparent receives a free meal during the day and an annual free physical examination.

HOME HANDYMAN

This program provides free or low cost home repair services to isolated elderly. The maintenance and repair work is done by elderly retirees.

There are sometimes other support services like this one provided as part of Retired Senior Volunteer Programs (RSVP).

MEALS ON WHEELS PROGRAM

Meals are delivered to elderly who are unable to prepare or afford a nutritious meal. One hot meal and one cold meal are provided per day at a nominal cost. There are also Senior Citizen Nutrition Programs located throughout the local community where nutritious meals are served twice daily for a donation amount decided by the person.

TELEPHONE LIFE LINE SERVICE

This is a daily friendly telephone call to elderly who live alone. The call is made at a designated time each day such that the older person comes to expect the supportive voice.

In addition to the above and to the services provided by general hospitals, nursing homes, and psychiatric facilities, most communities have the following programs available to adults, including elderly:

Alcohol-drug abuse programs
Arthritis and pain clinics
Heart clubs and the American Heart Association
Home Health Care Services
Craft and social programs
Consumer's rights organizations
Legal services (some communities have legal aid groups that are at low or no cost to the poor or to poor elderly)

On page 154 listing of American organizations pertaining to the elderly is provided. By far the largest of these is the combination of the American Association of Retired Persons (AARP) with the National Retired Teachers Association (NRTA). There are over 6 million persons over age 55 who are members. AARP/NRTA is dedicated to helping older American citizens achieve retirement lives of independence, purpose, and dignity. The two associations provide legislative representation of older persons at all levels of government, offer services to encourage elderly participation in community and public affairs, and publish magazines and other materials of special interest to older persons. The main publication of AARP/NRTA is the magazine, *Modern Maturity*, but special materials on church relations, consumer affairs, crime prevention, intergenerational alliance, health education, lifetime learning, safety, tax aids, and services for widowed persons can be obtained from AARP/NRTA at the address given.

The National Gerontological Society is the professional organization for those who deliver services, provide training, or develop knowledge through research. It is a multidisciplinary society consisting of planners, physicians, social workers, nurses, psychologists, and academicians from practically all disciplines, and many others. There are over 6000 members. *The Gerontologist* and the *Journal of Gerontology* are the two publications of the Gerontological Society and all members receive both these journals. Other large professional organizations in the United States sometimes have special interest groups concerned with aging. For example, members of Division 20 of the American Psychological Association have academic or applied interests in the psychological aspects of adult development and aging.

Some of the organizations listed below represent special groups of elderly. For example, the National Center for Black Aged and the National Caucus on Black Aged represent the interests of minority elderly in America. The Gray Panthers is an activist group founded by Maggie Kuhn which is committed to expanding the rights and opportunities of elderly. In most cases further information about an organization and its goals can be obtained by writing directly to the address provided.

This appendix concludes with a list of those National Groups concerned with health that are considered to be relevant to the welfare of the elderly.

ADDRESSES OF ORGANIZATIONS PERTAINING TO THE ELDERLY

ACTION
806 Connecticut Ave., N.W.
Washington, D.C. 20525

ACTION sponsors the following programs:
Foster Grandparent Program
Retired Senior Volunteer Program (RSVP)
Service Corp of Retired Executives (SCORE)

Administration on Aging
330 C Street, S.W.
HEW South
Washington, D.C. 20201

Adult Education Association
1225 19th Street
Washington, D.C. 22036

American Association of Retired Persons
1909 K Street, N.W.
Washington, D.C. 20006

The American Geriatrics Society
10 Columbus Circle
New York, New York 10019

Division of Adult Development and Aging (Div. 20)
American Psychological Association
1200 17th Street, N.W.
Washington, D.C. 20036

The Gerontological Society
1 Dupont Circle
Washington, D.C. 20036

Gray Panthers
3700 Chestnut Street
Philadelphia, Pennsylvania 19104

The National Association of Retired Federal Employees (NARFE)
1533 New Hampshire Avenue, N.W.
Washington, D.C. 20036

Suite 811
Washington, D.C. 20036

National Center on Black Aged
1730 M Street, N.W.
Suite 811
Washington, D.C. 20036

National Council on the Aging
1828 L Street, N.W.
Suite 504
Washington, D.C. 20036

National Council of Senior Citizens
1511 K Street, N.W.
Washington, D.C. 20005

This organization sponsors the Senior AIDES program. They offer reduced-cost programs for travel, prescription medication, and insurance.

National Institute on Aging
National Institutes of Health
Public Health Service
Bethesda, Maryland 20014

National Retired Teachers Association
1909 K Street, N.W.
Washington, D.C. 20006

New York City Department for the Aging
Central Office
250 Broadway
30th and 17th Floors
New York, New York 10007

(This department has established several model programs for the elderly in New York City including a Crime Prevention Program, advocacy, and information referral.)
Task Force on Older Women of the National Organization for Women (NOW)
3800 Harrison Street
Oakland, California 94611

NATIONAL GROUPS CONCERNED WITH HEALTH

Alcoholics Anonymous
PO Box 459
New York, N.Y. 10017

Alexander Graham Bell Association for the Deaf
3417 Volta Place, N.W.
Washington, D.C. 20007

Allergy Foundation of America
801 Second Avenue
New York, N.Y. 10017

American Academy of Family Physicians
1740 W. 92nd St.
Kansas City
Mo. 64114

American Cancer Society
777 Third Avenue
New York, N.Y. 10017

American Dental Association
211 E. Chicago Avenue
Chicago, Ill. 60611

American Diabetes Association
1W 48th St.
New York, N.Y. 10020

American Foundation for the Blind
15W 16th St.
New York, N.Y. 10011

American Heart Association
44E 23rd St.
New York, N.Y. 10010

American Lung Association
1740 Broadway
New York, N.Y. 10019

American Medical Association
535 N. Dearborn St.
Chicago, Ill. 60610

American Psychiatric Association
1700 18th St.
N.W. Washington, D.C. 20009

American Red Cross
17th and D Sts., N.W.
Washington, D.C. 20006

American Speech and Hearing Association
9030 Old Georgetown Rd.
Bethesda, Md 20014

Arthritis Foundation
475 Riverside Drive
New York, N.Y. 10027

Braille Institute of America
741 N. Vermont Avenue
Los Angeles, California 90029

Family Service Association of America
44 East 23rd St.
New York, N.Y. 10010

National Institute of Mental Health
5600 Fishers Ln.
Rockville, Md. 20852

National Kidney Foundation
116 E. 27th St.
New York, N.Y. 10016

National Parkinson Foundation
1501 N.W. Ninth Avenue
Miami, Florida 33136

National Society for the Prevention of Blindness
79 Madison Avenue
New York, N.Y. 10016

SIECUS
(Sex Information and Education Council of the U.S.)
1855 Broadway
New York, N.Y. 10023

Index